The
WORKING
COOK

Fun, Fresh, Fast, and Healthful Recipes for Everyday Easy Cooking

Lou Seibert Pappas

BETTERWAY PUBLICATIONS, INC.
WHITE HALL, VIRGINIA

Also by the same author:

Winemakers Cookbook
The New Harvest
New American Chefs
Entertaining in the Light Style
From Sea to Stream
Vegetable Cookery
Greek Cooking
Party Menus
Gourmet Cooking the Slim Way
Entertaining the Slim Way

The
WORKING
COOK

Fun, Fresh, Fast, and Healthful Recipes for Everyday Easy Cooking

Lou Seibert Pappas

BETTERWAY PUBLICATIONS, INC.
WHITE HALL, VIRGINIA

Published by Betterway Publications, Inc.
P.O. Box 219
Crozet, VA 22932
(804) 823-5661

Cover design by Rick Britton
Cover photograph and insert photographs by Renee Lynn
Typography by Typecasting

Pappas, Lou Seibert.
    The working cook: fun, fresh, fast, and healthful recipes for everyday easy cooking / Lou Seibert Pappas.
        p.   cm.
    Includes index.
    ISBN 1-55870-191-5 (pbk.): $14.95
    1. Quick and easy cookery. I. Title.
TX833.5.P37   1991
641.5'12—dc20   90-21736
                                                                 CIP

Printed in the United States of America
0 9 8 7 6 5 4 3 2 1

Contents

Introduction

Time is a precious commodity for the working cook. The freedom to spend hours in the kitchen creating dinner is a luxury for most. Instead, the daily format for most busy working cooks is about a half-hour to prepare each weekday meal. The dual demands of straddling a career and a chef's hat pose a challenge for millions.

One way to meet this challenge is to zero in on dishes that are fun, fast, fresh, and healthy. This way the meal can be delicious and rewarding to the cook and diners alike.

Our busy contemporary lifestyles have inspired a whole new formula for dining. No longer is a meal with meat, starch, and side vegetables the custom on the dinner plate. Rather, it is the exception, as we embrace exciting, innovative fare like full-meal soups, hot and cold main course salads, plate-size tortilla pizzas, seafood-rippled pastas, and plump cheese-filled omelets. Poultry and fish are important elements in our new diet, and fresh produce is essential. Ethnic dishes lend a wealth of variety to our repertoire and stimulate our palates with new taste sensations.

Simplicity with an air of sophistication is the norm of the working cook in the '90s, and surprise is a special bonus. We are discovering that it takes just a few flavor-packed ingredients to lend a whole new dimension to everyday fare.

The new genies in the kitchen are the wonderful fresh herbs such as basil, rosemary, tarragon, thyme, and mint; the long-time staples such as ginger root, garlic, and shallots; and such ethnic exotic seasonings as lemon grass and jalapeños. The range of oils — virgin olive oil, sesame, walnut, and hazelnut oil; the various vinegars — from raspberry, sherry, and balsamic to wine herb — punctuate salads and sauces with their keen, clear overtones. Choice fresh produce has expanded multi-fold with new taste treats in imported fruits and a whole new range of varieties in such everyday staples as apples, salad greens, melons, and squash. With seafood from around the world and other numerous bounty at hand, delicious dining relies on these ingredients prepared with a light, deft hand.

For variety and excitement in our daily fare, our menus have taken on a worldly format as we travel the globe savoring ethnic dishes. Stir-fries, satays, pizza, pastas, curries, tajines, and terrines are becoming commonplace.

The smart weekday cook utilizes the weekend as a bonus time for clever make-ahead house staples. These encompass nourishing full-meal soups, aromatic breads, tantalizing cookies and cakes, versatile meat sauces, handy terrines, and mini meat loaves to slide between a sandwich to fill a lunch bag or adorn the dinner plate. A great house salad dressing, yogurt cheese, pesto, and salsas lend flair and personality to the menu pattern. The clever cook can package items in daily portions for the freezer, ready for quick cooking in the microwave, and have almost instant dining.

After all, though commercial frozen entrées and fast food are convenient, they do not satisfy the soul like special condiments, home-baked sweets, and the many savories the home cook can provide.

The weekday cook takes advantage of bonus dishes. They may evolve from a barbecued entrée, such as a butterflied leg of lamb, lemon-basted turkey breast, grilled skirt steak, or gingered pork roast. After savoring the hot grilled item one night, the next day's meal can feature the surplus in a main dish salad, a pasta dish, or tortilla—rolled for fajitas or open-face for a pizza.

The fresh herbs we now prize may come from a sunny backyard garden, a kitchen window sill, the local farmer's market, or the greengrocer. Whatever the source, the sprigs are indispensable to uplifting many dishes.

Contemplating our food trends and dining patterns, it is the simplicity of a dish that really counts now, accented with the pizzazz of a flavor-packed fresh seasoning—that feather of dill, sprig of tarragon, splash of raspberry vinegar, or dollop of fruity olive oil. These little touches reward and satisfy our taste buds with ongoing delight and pleasure.

Many of the recipes in this book are designed for two. These recipes can easily be doubled or tripled to accommodate the number of diners.

With time the dilemma of the working cook, shortcuts are in order and easy, ethnic fare with ultra-fresh ingredients is my secret to delicious everyday variety at the table.

Lou Seibert Pappas
Palo Alto, California

The Pantry Essentials

A well-stocked pantry is a boon to the working cook. It brings freedom for creative cooking, both as a daily routine and in an impromptu fashion if guests are invited spontaneously.

Every good cook has a list of favorite ingredients that are always on hand. Besides such basics as sugar, flour, rice, pasta, eggs, and milk, here are ones that are essential to any good kitchen:

PANTRY

Ginger root; garlic; red and yellow onions; potatoes, both baking and new; lemons and oranges, for both the versatile zest and the juice.

Extra-virgin olive oil, sesame oil, walnut and hazelnut oils, canola oil.

Balsamic vinegar; rice wine vinegar; other flavored wine, fruit, and herb vinegars.

Bulgur, couscous, wild rice, gourmet brown rice, black beans, lentils, and split peas.

Canned tomato paste, anchovies, grape leaves, and garbanzo beans. Canned chicken broth, bouillon cubes, or homemade frozen stock.

Brown sugar and honey.

Semisweet chocolate, unsweetened chocolate, white chocolate chips, and cocoa.

Jams and jellies: apricot, orange marmalade, strawberry, and raspberry. Cassis (black currant) syrup and crystallized ginger.

Sun-dried tomatoes, preferably homemade, stocked in the freezer. Dried wild mushrooms.

Capers, chutney, Worcestershire sauce, hot pepper sauce, soy sauce, and a variety of mustards, with Dijon a must.

Nuts: almonds, walnuts, pecans, pistachios, and roasted sunflower seeds. (Store any of these in the freezer if you must keep them for any length of time.)

Packages of active dry yeast, whole wheat flour, and cornmeal.

Herb essentials to stand in when fresh herbs are unavailable: basil, dill, tarragon, thyme. Madras curry powder. Herbes de Provence, saffron threads, sweet and hot paprikas, hot chili peppers. Spices: cinnamon, whole nutmeg to grind, anise seed, ground allspice.

REFRIGERATOR STAPLES

Cheeses, including a chunk of Parmesan, a blue such as Gorgonzola or Blue Castello which ages well, and a Swiss-type or Jarlsberg. Optional cheeses are Monterey Jack and a cheddar.

Granny Smith or Golden Delicious apples, carrots, celery, and greens for salad making.

FREEZER ITEMS

Ice cream (vanilla bean and toasted almond flavors), frozen yogurt, and raspberry sherbet.

Homemade breads, cookies, and cakes.

Soups packaged in 1-pint containers.

Poultry and fish: 1-pound packages of ground turkey; whole broiler-fryers, about 3-pound size; frozen trout and snapper, for emergencies.

Whole wheat, flour, and corn tortillas.

WINES AND LIQUEURS

Sherry, port, and brandy for flavoring soups, enriching sauces, and enhancing desserts.

Dark Jamaica rum and Kahlua.

Grand Marnier or Cointreau, framboise, Frangelico, and crème de cassis.

The Working Cook's Menus

SHELLFISH SUNDOWN SUPPER

Greens with Shallot Vinaigrette
Fisherman's Shellfish Platter
Rhubarb and Strawberry Bowls

ROAST CHICKEN FOR GUESTS

Mushroom Fennel Salad
Roast Chicken with Grapes
Broccoli Flowerets
Brandied Apple Slices with Ice Cream

MYKONOS SOUP SUPPER

Avgolemono Soup with Pistachios
Shrimp and Grape Leaf Salad Plate
Stuffed Apricots with Honey Gingered Cheese

A FISH SURPRISE DINNER

Parsley Salad
Leek and Snapper Packets
Brown Rice
Winter Pears Helene

AN ARMENIAN PIZZA SUPPER

Mediterranean Fruit Salad
Armenian Pizzas
Frozen Yogurt from the Market

AN EVERYDAY CLASSIC

Layered Gazpacho Salad
Joe's Special
Toasted French Bread
White Chocolate and Pistachio Chipperoos

A BRITTANY FISH SUPPER

Greens with Shallot Vinaigrette
Brittany Fish Stew
Lemon Custard Soufflé

A FAST PASTA SPREAD

Fruited Blue Cheese Salad Plate
Angel Hair Pasta with Smoked Salmon and Basil
Biscotti

BROWN BAGS BANDIT-STYLE

Spicy Spinach Salad
Lamb Bandit Style
Grand Marnier Ice Cream

AN ITALIAN TAKE-OFF

Tomatoes with Pesto
Turkey Spiedini
Shredded Zucchini
Iced Coffee Floats

JUST MUSHROOMS

Greens with Enokis and Toasted Walnuts
Baked Mushrooms with Chèvre
Carrots Orangerie
Strawberries with Cassis

A FAST GUEST DINNER

Vintner's Broth
Chicken Breasts with Chèvre and Sun-Dried Tomatoes
Green Beans with Tarragon
White Chocolate Velvet

A SALAD SUPPER

Crab-Stuffed Artichokes
Papaya Fruit Plate

A CRÊPE AFFAIR

Green Salad with Pistachios
Buckwheat Galettes with Ham and Cheese
Strawberries in Wine

A FAMILY PARTY

Gingered Vichyssoise
Fillets with Gorgonzola
Asparagus with Pine Nuts
Chocolate Almond Torte

A SUMMER SUPPER

Gingered Carrot Soup
Pistachio-Studded Chicken Terrine
Garden Relishes with Herb Yogurt Cheese
Ruby Fruit Compote

A MOROCCAN TREAT

Pickled Vegetables
Veal and Apricots Tajine
Spicy Couscous
Honey Ice Cream

A GUEST DINNER

Green Salad with Mushrooms
Five Spice Game Hen with Fruit
Steamed White and Wild Rice
Lemon Shells with Lemon Ice

Appetizers and First Courses

For the working cook, appetizers that go together in a jiffy or that can be made in advance are in demand. Some of the zestful vegetable spreads on these pages can be prepared ahead and kept refrigerated for two to three days, such as Shiitake Mushroom Walnut Pâté, Sunchoke and Pistachio Spread, or Eggplant Sunflower Seed Spread. Other appetizers, like the Peppered Herb Cheese and the Tapénade, keep well refrigerated for up to a week.

Impromptu appetizers that can be swiftly made at the last minute include Mango and Green Chili Tortilla Bites, Vegetable Skewers, and Chile Con Queso.

Some appetizers can also serve as a light entrée. For these consider Mushroom Mini-Frittatas, French Appetizer Tart, or Raclette with Spuds, Sausage, and Fennel.

Peppered Herb Cheese

Herbs and red chili peppers imbue cheese with zestful spunk for a fast appetizer.

8 ounces Monterey Jack, fontina,
    Muenster, or semi-soft low-fat
    cheese
2 tablespoons fresh mixed herbs:
    thyme, oregano, and rosemary
1 dried hot red chili pepper, split

1 bay leaf
Virgin olive oil (about 1 cup)
Thin wheat crackers
Fennel stalks or sliced mushrooms,
    for accompaniment

Cut cheese into 1¼-inch cubes and place in a wide-mouthed jar. Sprinkle with herbs. Add chili pepper and bay leaf. Pour in oil to just cover cheese. Cover the jar and let it stand in the refrigerator for 3 or 4 days.

To serve, place pieces of cheese on small plates with thin wheat crackers. For an additional flavor treat, accompany the cheese with pieces of fennel or slices of mushrooms. Makes 6 to 8 servings.

Melons and Meats

The renowned Italian appetizer, melon with prosciutto, makes a fine starting point for matching various melon varieties and cold sliced sausages and meats.

On each plate, arrange 2 or 3 thin slices of melon and overlap them with thin slices of prosciutto on top.

Other good combinations to try are:

Crenshaw melon, Lebanon bologna, and sliced avocado with lime wedges

Honeydew and dry salami or prosciutto

Cantaloupe and pastrami, Thuringer, or mortadella

Persian melon and Westphalian ham with sliced avocado and lemon wedges

Mango and Green Chili Tortilla Bites

This is an exotic hot appetizer that goes together in a jiffy.

6 (6-inch) flour tortillas
2 cups (8 ounces) shredded
    Monterey Jack cheese

1 can (4 ounces) diced green chilies
1 mango, peeled, thinly sliced,
    and cut in 1-inch pieces

Sprinkle 3 tortillas with half of the cheese. Scatter the chilies over the cheese and arrange mango pieces on top. Then cover the tortillas with the remaining cheese and top with remaining tortillas. Grill in a large hot skillet, carefully turning to brown both sides. Cook until heated through and cheese is melted. Transfer the tortillas to a board, cut in wedges, and serve. Makes 18 appetizers.

Quesadillas

These cheese-filled tortillas are easily assembled ahead of time, ready for last-minute grilling.

1 can (7 ounces) chilies, seeded and chopped
¾ pound Monterey Jack, Muenster, or cheddar cheese, coarsely shredded

2½ dozen small (4-inch) corn or flour tortillas

In a bowl, mix the chilies and cheese together lightly. Spoon a mound of the mixture on each tortilla, fold in half, and skewer with a toothpick. Heat the tortillas in an ungreased frying pan, turning and cooking them until just heated through and cheese is melted. (Or fry in unsalted butter or oil, if desired.) Makes 2½ dozen appetizers.

Chili con Queso

This is an easy-to-assemble hot Mexican appetizer.

1 small onion, finely chopped
1 tablespoon olive oil
1 medium tomato, peeled and
   chopped

2 canned green chili peppers,
   seeded and chopped
½ pound teleme cheese or cheddar
   cheese, sliced
Small hot tortilla chips

Using a small combination skillet-serving dish, sauté onions in oil until golden brown. Add tomatoes and peppers and sauté until the vegetables are glazed. Add the cheese and heat just until melted. Keep the dip warm over a candle warmer or hot tray and serve with a basket of chips. Makes about 8 appetizer servings.

Sunchoke and Pistachio Spread

Sunchokes, also known as Jerusalem artichokes, lend a distinctive nutty flavor to this attractive light cream-colored spread.

3 cloves garlic
½ teaspoon olive oil
12 ounces sunchokes
2 teaspoons lemon juice
1 teaspoon fresh oregano or thyme
     or ¼ teaspoon dried oregano
     or thyme

2 tablespoons chopped parsley
1 shallot, chopped
⅓ cup Yogurt Cheese (see page 248)
     or 3 ounces natural cream
     cheese
3 tablespoons salted pistachio nuts
Sesame crackers or raw relishes

Cut the stem end from each garlic clove but leave the peel on. Place on a sheet of foil and drizzle with oil. Wrap tightly and bake in a preheated 400° oven for 15 minutes or until soft. Place the sunchokes in a saucepan with water, cover, and simmer until tender, about 20 to 30 minutes. Drain and cool. Then peel the sunchokes and purée them in a blender or food processor with the lemon juice, oregano, parsley, shallot, and Yogurt Cheese. Squeeze the garlic cloves from their skins, add to the sunchokes and purée. Reserve 1 teaspoon of nuts for garnish. Add remaining nuts and blend just until chopped. Spoon the spread into a container and chill. Serve with sesame crackers or raw vegetables such as halved cherry tomatoes, button mushroom caps, diagonally sliced carrots, zucchini, or jicama. Makes about 1½ cups.

Tomato and Basil Cheese Spread

Sun-dried tomatoes, basil, and garlic lend pizzazz to this spread to top toasted baguettes. The spread may also be used on raw vegetables and baked potatoes, or a dollop may top broiled fish.

1 cup Yogurt Cheese (see page 248)
⅓ cup snipped sun-dried tomatoes
2 tablespoons chopped basil

Dash salt and freshly ground
* pepper, to taste*
2 cloves garlic, minced

First prepare Yogurt Cheese. In a bowl, mix Yogurt Cheese with tomatoes, basil, salt and pepper, and garlic. Cover and refrigerate 2 hours for flavors to blend. Serve as a spread on toasted baguettes. Makes 1½ cups.

Eggplant Sunflower Seed Spread

An herb-sparked eggplant spread can serve as an appetizer or a first course ringed with red and gold plum tomatoes or two or three stuffed grape leaves.

1 large eggplant, about 1¼ pounds
¼ pound shiitake or button
    mushrooms, chopped
2 shallots, chopped
1 tablespoon olive oil
2 tablespoons lemon juice
3 cloves garlic, minced
Salt and freshly ground black
    pepper, to taste

⅓ cup low-fat yogurt
1 tablespoon chopped fresh basil
3 tablespoons chopped Italian
    parsley
Romaine leaves, for garnish
¼ cup toasted sunflower seeds
Nicoise olives, for garnish
    (optional)
Lavosh or sesame crackers

Place the whole eggplant in a baking pan and bake, uncovered, in a pre-heated 400° oven for 30 to 40 minutes or until soft. (Or microwave on high for 10 minutes or until soft.) Dip the eggplant into cold water, prick with a fork, and squeeze out the juices. Then peel it and let it cool. Purée the eggplant in a food processor or blender. Sauté the mushrooms and shallots in oil until glazed and add to the eggplant. Add lemon juice and garlic and purée. Season with salt and pepper and stir in the yogurt, basil, and parsley. Turn the spread into a container, cover, and chill. When ready to serve, mound onto a plate lined with romaine spears and sprinkle with sunflower seeds. Surround the eggplant spread with olives, if desired. Serve with lavosh or sesame crackers. Makes 8 servings.

Garbanzo Sesame Dip

Sesame oil and cumin spark this Mediterranean bean dip. Lavosh makes a great scooper for it.

1 can (1 pound) garbanzo beans
⅓ cup lemon juice
2 garlic cloves, peeled
3 tablespoons chopped Italian
   parsley
1 tablespoon chopped green onion
   tops or chives
¼ teaspoon salt

¼ teaspoon ground cumin
Dash of pepper
1 tablespoon sesame oil
Italian parsley sprigs, for garnish
Lavosh, sesame, or oat crackers;
   or sliced cucumbers, zucchini,
   jicama, or carrots

Drain the garbanzo beans, reserving the liquid. Place the beans, lemon juice, garlic, parsley, onion tops, salt, cumin, pepper, and sesame oil into a food processor fitted with a steel blade. Process until almost smooth. If the mixture is too stiff, add a little reserved bean liquid. Spoon the spread into a serving container. Cover and chill. To serve, garnish with parsley sprigs and accompany with lavosh, crackers, or relishes. Makes about 2 cups.

Herb Cheese Dip

Fresh herbs enhance homemade Yogurt Cheese for a flavorful low calorie dip or spread. It also makes an excellent topping for baked potatoes and fresh steamed vegetables such as asparagus, green beans, or carrots.

¾ cup Yogurt Cheese (see
   page 248)
1 shallot, chopped
1 clove garlic, minced
¼ cup chopped parsley
1 tablespoon fresh chopped
   tarragon or ¼ teaspoon dried
   tarragon

Salt and pepper, to taste
1 teaspoon Dijon or Parisian
   mustard
Assorted vegetables: jicama,
   mushrooms, sugar peas,
   carrots, radishes, zucchini

Place the Yogurt Cheese in a bowl. Add the shallots, garlic, parsley, tarragon, salt, pepper, and mustard and mix to blend. Serve in a bowl surrounded by assorted vegetables. If desired, arrange the vegetables in a basket like a nosegay. Makes 1 cup.

Tapénade

A zestful herb and anchovy mayonnaise, this tapénade is a versatile sauce for cooked artichokes and other vegetables and a dressing for salad combinations of greens and seafood. Or serve it in small ramekins to accompany a platter salad of cooked shrimp, sliced fennel, cantaloupe wedges, and cherry tomatoes.

1 egg
1½ tablespoons lemon juice
1½ tablespoons white wine vinegar
1 teaspoon salt
1 teaspoon sugar
1 teaspoon dry mustard

1 cup canola or safflower oil
3 tablespoons capers
1 clove garlic, minced
6 anchovy fillets
3 tablespoons chopped parsley
½ teaspoon grated lemon peel

Place the egg, lemon juice, vinegar, salt, sugar, and mustard in a blender or food processor fitted with the steel blade. Blend for a few seconds. With motor turned on, gradually pour in the oil in a slow, steady stream and blend until smooth. Add capers, garlic, anchovies, parsley, and lemon peel and blend just until minced. Turn into a container, cover, and chill until serving time. Makes about 1½ cups.

Vegetable Skewers

Skewered vegetables make a fun appetizer or a colorful accompaniment for meat.

*8 stuffed grape leaves, homemade
   or canned (see page 249)*
8 mushroom caps

8 cherry tomatoes
8 marinated artichoke hearts

Alternate the vegetables on 8 skewers; chill. Makes 8 appetizers or 4 side accompaniments to an entrée.

Shiitake Mushroom Walnut Pâté

Let this robust mushroom spread serve as an ideal appetizer for an entrée
of roast chicken or game birds.

⅓ cup walnuts
2 tablespoons butter or olive oil
2 shallots, finely chopped
½ pound shiitake mushrooms or
    button mushrooms, chopped
1 clove garlic, minced
2 teaspoons lemon juice
1 teaspoon fresh tarragon, chopped

Salt and pepper, to taste
2 tablespoons minced Italian
    parsley
2 tablespoons sour cream
2 tablespoons plain yogurt
Italian parsley sprigs or chive
    blossoms, for garnish
Sesame crackers or lavosh

Spread nuts in a shallow pan and bake in a preheated 300° oven for 10 to
15 minutes or until lightly toasted. Let the nuts cool and finely chop them.
Melt the butter in a large skillet over medium heat, add shallots and sauté
for 2 to 3 minutes. Add the mushrooms, garlic, and lemon juice and cook
until soft. With a slotted spoon transfer the mushroom mixture to a bowl
and mix in the tarragon, salt, and pepper. Cook down any remaining pan
juices until reduced to a glaze and spoon over the mushrooms. Add nuts,
parsley, sour cream, and yogurt. Using a food processor fitted with a steel
blade, process the mixture until nearly smooth. Spoon into a serving container, cover, and refrigerate for 2 hours or longer for flavors to blend.
Garnish with parsley sprigs or chive blossoms. Serve with crackers. Makes
about 1⅓ cups.

Stuffed Grape Leaves with Crabmeat and Yogurt Cheese

This exciting appetizer is fast to assemble with grape leaves for the wrapper.

1 cup Yogurt Cheese (see page 248)
1½ teaspoons grated lemon zest
2 tablespoons lemon juice
⅓ cup finely chopped parsley
½ teaspoon dried tarragon
¾ pound crabmeat or surimi
  (artificial crabmeat)

2 tablespoons currants or golden
  raisins
18 grape leaves (approximately),
  rinsed
Cherry tomatoes, for garnish
Lemon wedges, for garnish

The day before you plan to serve this, prepare the Yogurt Cheese.

In a bowl, mix together the lemon zest, lemon juice, parsley, tarragon, crabmeat, and currants. Let the mixture marinate for 15 minutes. Mix in the Yogurt Cheese. Lay the grape leaves flat on a board. Place a tablespoon of the crab mixture just above the stem end of a grape leaf. Fold in sides and roll up making a neat packet. Repeat. Chill the grape leaves for 2 hours. Arrange them on a platter, garnish with cherry tomatoes and lemon wedges. Makes 18 appetizers.

Raclette with Spuds, Sausage, and Fennel

Raclette is a Swiss dish traditionally eaten by dipping or scooping the potatoes in the melted cheese. It is a fast appetizer that can also double as an entrée for two.

*4 ounces Gruyère, Samsoe, or
    Jarlsberg cheese
8 tiny new potatoes (red, purple,
    or gold or an assortment)*

*8 cocktail sausages
½ fennel bulb, trimmed and sliced*

Thinly slice cheese and place in a 9-inch pie plate. Heat in a preheated 350° oven until cheese is melted and starts to brown, about 10 minutes. Meanwhile, microwave potatoes on high 5 to 6 minutes or until tender. Heat sausages in the microwave oven until heated through, about 2 minutes. Divide the cheese among 4 appetizer plates and surround each serving with 2 potatoes, 2 sausages, and some sliced fennel. Makes 4 servings.

Quick Wine Cheese Puff

This golden brown cheese puff can serve double duty as an appetizer or light entrée accompaniment to a soup or salad supper.

3 eggs
⅔ cup all-purpose flour
⅓ cup dry white wine
⅔ cup milk
¼ teaspoon salt
2 teaspoons Dijon mustard

1 shallot or green onion, finely
   chopped
1 cup grated Jarlsberg or Swiss
   cheese, or low-fat Swiss cheese
1 tablespoon butter, melted
2 tablespoons grated Parmesan or
   Romano cheese

Beat the eggs until light and mix in flour, wine, milk, salt, and mustard, mixing until blended. Add shallot, Jarlsberg cheese, and butter. Pour into a buttered 9-inch pie pan and sprinkle with Parmesan cheese. Bake in a preheated 425° oven for 30 to 35 minutes or until puffed and golden brown. Cut in wedges. Makes about 1 dozen appetizers or 6 entrée servings.

Mushroom Mini-Frittatas

Mushrooms, green onions, and cheese enrich mini-frittatas for bite-size appetizers.

1 teaspoon olive oil
1 bunch green onions, chopped
   (approximately 1½ cups)
¼ pound mushrooms, sliced
2 cloves garlic, minced
8 soft sun-dried tomato halves, cut
   in pieces

4 eggs
⅓ cup plain low-fat yogurt
¼ cup chopped parsley
½ teaspoon dried tarragon
Dash of salt and pepper, to taste
½ cup shredded Jarlsberg or
   Gruyère cheese

In a medium-sized skillet, heat oil over medium heat, add onions and sauté until glazed. Add mushrooms, garlic, and tomato halves and sauté 1 minute. Remove from heat. Beat eggs until blended and mix in yogurt, parsley, tarragon, and salt and pepper. Stir in mushroom mixture. Lightly oil 16 small muffin cups or spray with non-stick spray. Spoon in the egg mixture, filling each cup. Sprinkle cheese on top. Bake in a preheated 425° oven for 10 minutes or until just set. Remove from heat, let cool 2 minutes, and remove from pans. Serve hot. If desired, make in advance and reheat in a microwave oven. Makes 16 appetizers.

Shrimp Triangles

Either shrimp or surimi crab makes a flavorful, plump stuffing for crispy filo triangles. A big batch can be assembled in advance, frozen, and then baked for impromptu serving.

8 ounces low-fat cream cheese, at
   room temperature
1 egg
¼ cup chopped parsley
2 green onions, finely chopped
1 teaspoon freshly grated lemon
   zest
1 teaspoon chopped fresh tarragon
   or ¼ teaspoon dried tarragon

Dash of Worcestershire sauce
½ pound small cooked shrimp or
   crabmeat
⅓ cup grated Parmesan cheese
½ cup grated low-fat Monterey
   Jack cheese
About 8 sheets filo dough
6 tablespoons unsalted or clarified
   butter, melted

Beat cream cheese until creamy and mix in egg, parsley, onions, lemon zest, tarragon, Worcestershire sauce, shrimp, and cheeses. Mix just until evenly distributed. Lay out 1 sheet of filo dough (keep remaining sheets covered with plastic wrap so they will not dry out) and lightly brush with melted butter. Cut crosswise into 3-inch wide strips. Place a rounded teaspoon of cheese filling on a narrow end of each strip and fold over one corner. Continue folding pastry from side to side like a flag, making a triangle. Place on a lightly buttered baking sheet. Proceed in this manner with remaining filo and filling. Brush tops of triangles with melted butter. (If desired, freeze at this point, tightly covered. Let thaw at room temperature before baking.) Bake in a preheated 350° oven for 15 minutes, or until golden brown. Serve hot. Makes about 4 dozen.

Hint: The shrimp triangles may be frozen for up to 1 month.

French Appetizer Tart

This decorative first-course tart can have endless filling variations. Consider ripe olives, caviar, and minced hard-cooked eggs or vary the pattern with shrimp or crabmeat. Let the tart serve as an elegant entrée as well, with a bountiful green salad and a cool soup starter.

Savory Crust (recipe follows)
1 cup Yogurt Cheese (see page 248)
2 tablespoons chopped shallots
3 tablespoons chopped Italian
     parsley

Salt and pepper, to taste
½ teaspoon grated lemon zest
2 to 3 ounces sliced smoked salmon
3 hard-cooked eggs
2 green onions, chopped

Prepare Savory Crust (see below).

In a bowl, mix together the Yogurt Cheese, shallots, parsley, salt, pepper, and lemon zest. Spread the cheese mixture into the baked tart shell. Cut the salmon in small strips and arrange around outer ring of tart. Peel the eggs, separate yolks and whites, and finely chop whites and shred yolks. Make a ring of whites just inside salmon and follow with a ring of chopped onions and a circle of yolks in the center. Cover and chill until ready to serve. Makes 10 first course servings or 6 entrée servings.

SAVORY BUTTER CRUST:

1 cup all-purpose flour
1 teaspoon grated lemon zest

4 ounces (1 stick) butter, cut into
     8 pieces
1 egg yolk

Place the flour, lemon zest, and butter in a mixing bowl and cut in the butter until the mixture is crumbly. Mix in the egg yolk and form dough into a ball. Pat dough onto bottom and sides of an 11-inch fluted flan pan with removable bottom. Place in the freezer for 10 minutes to firm up. Bake in a preheated 425° oven for 8 to 10 minutes or until golden brown. Makes an 11-inch pastry crust.

Soups

Soups can work magic in the busy cook's pantry. They are naturals for make-ahead preparation and storing in the freezer. They can be packaged in handy-to-thaw and easy-to-reheat containers. Divided into bowls, soups are swiftly microwaved for fast table service.

The fresh vegetable combinations such as Leek and Sunchoke Soup, Gingered Carrot Soup, and Golden Squash Pesto Soup can make an uplifting and decorative first course. For an added touch, garnish them with fresh herbs.

Other soups are full meal dishes, such as Moroccan Meatball Soup, Lentil and Sausage Soup, Chicken and White Bean Soup, and Early California Soup. These can be made in quantity, ready to use for several meals.

The fish soups and stews such as Brittany Fish Stew are designed for freshly purchased seafood, cooked and served the same day.

For those with a yearning for a healthful, traditional vegetable soup, Provencal Vegetable Soup au Pistou or Bistro Potage fill the bill.

Frosty Avocado Soup

This cool summer soup goes together in a jiffy and can be served with a variety of garnish toppings.

1 medium-sized avocado, peeled and halved
2 cups buttermilk or plain yogurt
2 teaspoons lemon juice

Dash of liquid hot pepper seasoning
Cantaloupe balls, papaya cubes, or small cooked shrimp, and yogurt, for garnish

Place the avocado, buttermilk, lemon juice, and liquid hot pepper seasoning in a blender. Blend until smooth. Pour the mixture into a container, cover, and chill 1 hour. To serve, pour into small bowls and top with melon balls, papaya, or shrimp, and a dollop of yogurt. Makes 4 servings.

Vintner's Broth

A dollop of pesto lends a fragrant flourish to a wine-scented broth.

1 tablespoon olive oil
⅓ cup grated Parmesan or Romano
   cheese
1 clove garlic, minced
2 tablespoons finely chopped fresh
   basil

2 teaspoons finely chopped Italian
   parsley
3½ cups beef broth
½ cup dry red wine

Mix together the olive oil, cheese, garlic, basil, and parsley in a small bowl.
   Heat the broth and wine until steaming. Ladle into small bowls or cups and add a dollop of the basil mixture to each portion. Makes 6 servings.

Avgolemono Pistachio Soup

The Greek way of whisking lemon and eggs with chicken broth results in a remarkable low-calorie, yet filling soup.

3 cups chicken broth
1½ tablespoons cornstarch
1½ tablespoons cold water
3 eggs

¼ cup lemon juice
Lemon slices, for garnish
2 tablespoons chopped pistachios,
*   for garnish*

In a saucepan, heat chicken broth to boiling and stir in a paste of the cornstarch and water. Cook 2 minutes. Whisk together eggs and lemon juice and pour half the broth into the egg mixture, whisking constantly. Return to saucepan with remaining broth and cook over very low heat, stirring constantly, until thickened. Do not boil or soup will curdle. Ladle into soup bowls, small tea cups, or individual soufflé dishes and garnish with a lemon slice and chopped nuts. Makes 4 servings.

Maritata Soup

This creamy-rich Italian wedding soup makes an elegant pass-around starter.

2 tablespoons unsalted butter, at
    room temperature
½ cup grated fontina, Samsoe, or
    Monterey Jack cheese
¼ cup grated Romano or
    Parmesan cheese

2 egg yolks
½ cup heavy cream
3 cups chicken broth
½ cup dry white wine
Chopped chives or minced Italian
    parsley, for garnish

In a small bowl, beat together the butter, cheeses, and egg yolks. Gradually mix in the cream. In a large saucepan, heat chicken stock and wine to steaming. Mix a little hot stock into the cheese mixture, stirring constantly. Stir into the remaining broth in the pan. Heat through, stirring until blended. Ladle into small cups for sipping or use bowls for table service. Sprinkle with chives or parsley. Makes 6 servings.

Mustard Tarragon Soup

This zestful soup makes a conversation-starting first course for guests.

4 shallots, coarsely chopped
1 teaspoon olive oil
3 cups chicken broth
1 tablespoon chopped fresh
    tarragon or ¾ teaspoon dried
    tarragon
1 teaspoon fresh thyme or
    ¼ teaspoon dried thyme
2 tablespoons whole grain mustard
1 clove garlic, minced

¼ cup dry white wine
Salt and pepper, to taste
1 tablespoon cornstarch blended
    with 1 tablespoon water
⅓ cup heavy cream
Toasted baguette slices with
    Romano or Monterey Jack
    cheese topping, for
    accompaniment

In a saucepan, sauté shallots in oil until soft and slightly golden. Add broth, tarragon, thyme, mustard, garlic, wine, and salt and pepper, to taste. Bring to a boil and simmer 10 minutes. Add cornstarch paste and cook until thickened. Purée in a blender until smooth. Add cream and heat. Serve in mugs for pass-around style or in small bowls for a first course. Place grated Romano or Monterey Jack cheese on toasted baguette slices and broil just until the cheese melts. Serve with the soup. Makes 6 servings.

Gingered Carrot Soup

Ginger root lends a great spark to this colorful carrot soup.

3 cups chicken broth
1 large sweet onion, chopped
4 large carrots, peeled and cut in
  1-inch chunks
⅛ teaspoon ground nutmeg
2 teaspoons grated or chopped
  ginger root

1 clove garlic, minced
Dash liquid hot pepper seasoning
Salt and pepper, to taste
¼ cup dry white wine
Chopped parsley, chives, or diced
  red-skinned apple, for garnish

Place the chicken stock, onion, carrots, nutmeg, ginger root, garlic, and pepper seasoning in a saucepan. Cover and simmer until vegetables are very tender, about 20 minutes. Cool slightly and purée in a blender. Season with salt and pepper to taste. Return the soup to the saucepan, add wine, and heat through. Ladle into bowls and garnish with parsley, chives, or apple. Makes 4 servings.

Bistro Potage

Sunchokes, also known as Jerusalem artichokes, and shiitakes lend an unusual flavor to this creamy soup. Celery may be substituted for sunchokes if they are unavailable.

1 sweet Spanish onion, sliced
1 teaspoon olive oil
2 medium potatoes, peeled and
*   quartered*
3 medium carrots, peeled and cut
*   into chunks*
¼ pound sunchokes or 2 stalks
*   celery, cut in pieces*

4 dried shiitake mushrooms
1 quart chicken broth
1 tablespoon chopped parsley
Salt and pepper, to taste
Yogurt and chopped green onions,
*   for garnish*

In a soup pot, sauté onion in oil until glazed. Add potatoes, carrots, sunchokes, mushrooms, broth, and parsley. Cover and simmer until tender, about 30 to 40 minutes. Season with salt and pepper and purée in a blender. Serve hot, garnished with yogurt and green onions. Makes 6 servings.

Golden Squash Pesto Soup

This is a refreshing summer soup when squash is at its peak. Zucchini works equally well.

6 small yellow summer squash,
    thickly sliced
1 medium onion, chopped
2 cloves garlic, minced

3 cups chicken broth
Salt and pepper, to taste
⅓ cup Pesto Sauce (see page 243)
Yogurt and basil sprigs for garnish

In a large saucepan, simmer the squash, onion, and garlic in chicken broth with salt and pepper to taste, cooking until tender, about 20 minutes. Cool slightly, then purée in a blender or food processor. Add Pesto Sauce and blend again. Ladle into bowls. Garnish with yogurt and basil sprigs. Makes 4 to 6 servings.

Leek and Sunchoke Soup

The flavor duo of nutty sunchokes (Jerusalem artichokes) and caramelized leeks makes an unbeatable combination in this zestful soup. If counting calories, the cream may be omitted. When sunchokes are out of season, sweet potatoes may be substituted in this recipe (see note).

1 pound sunchokes
Juice of ½ lemon
2 teaspoons olive oil
1 large bunch leeks (white part
*   only), chopped*
1 medium onion, chopped
1 inner stalk celery, with leaves
1 clove garlic, chopped

4 cups chicken broth or 4 chicken
*   bouillon cubes and 4 cups water*
½ teaspoon dried tarragon
⅓ cup heavy cream (optional)
Salt and pepper, to taste
Yogurt and chopped pistachio nuts,
*   or parsley, for garnish*

Wash, peel, and slice sunchokes and drop them into a bowl of cold water with the juice of ½ lemon. In a large soup pot, heat the olive oil and sauté the leeks, onion, and celery, stirring occasionally, for about 10 minutes or until soft. Add sunchokes and garlic and sauté a few minutes longer. Add chicken broth and tarragon. Bring to a boil, cover, and simmer for 20 to 30 minutes or until sunchokes are tender. Let cool slightly. Purée in a blender with cream and season with salt and pepper to taste. Heat through and ladle into soup bowls. Garnish with a dollop of yogurt and sprinkle with pistachio nuts or parsley. Makes 6 servings.

Note: If desired, substitute 1 pound sweet potatoes, peeled and sliced, for the sunchokes and eliminate dropping them into lemon water.

Gingered Vichyssoise

Ginger enlivens this creamy vegetable soup that is excellent hot or cold.

1 tablespoon olive oil
1 onion, finely chopped
1 bunch leeks (white part only),
    sliced
2 teaspoons chopped fresh ginger
    root
2 cloves garlic, minced
1 quart chicken broth
1 large Yukon gold or baking
    potato, peeled and diced

2 teaspoons chopped fresh tarragon
    or ½ teaspoon dried tarragon
Salt and freshly ground pepper, to
    taste
¼ cup dry white wine
¼ cup heavy cream or plain
    low-fat yogurt
2 tablespoons finely chopped
    parsley, for garnish
Plain low-fat yogurt or sour
    cream, for garnish

In a large saucepan, heat the olive oil over moderate heat and sauté the onion, leeks, and ginger root until soft. Add garlic, chicken broth, potato, and tarragon and bring to a boil. Cover and simmer 20 minutes or until tender. Let cool slightly, then purée in a blender or food processor. Season with salt and pepper to taste. Blend in wine and cream. Cool and chill or serve hot. Garnish with parsley and a dollop of yogurt or sour cream. Makes 6 servings.

Provençal Vegetable Soup au Pistou

The first of the season young fresh vegetables are excellent in this aromatic soup. Accompany with crusty French bread and a fruit and cheese board.

1 quart chicken broth
4 small new potatoes, diced
2 small carrots, sliced
⅓ pound green beans or Italian beans, cut in 1-inch lengths
1 small zucchini, thinly sliced
1 yellow summer squash, thinly sliced

1 leek (white part only), sliced
⅓ cup shelled peas
2 cloves garlic, minced
2 Roma tomatoes, peeled and chopped
2 tablespoons chopped parsley
Pesto Sauce, for garnish (see page 243)

Using a large saucepan, heat the broth. Add the potatoes and carrots. Simmer 8 minutes. Add the beans, squash, and leek and simmer 5 minutes longer. Add the peas, garlic, tomatoes, and parsley and heat through. Ladle into soup bowls. Top with Pesto Sauce. Makes 4 servings.

Crab and Shrimp Soup

Use either fresh Dungeness or surimi crab for this succulent soup-stew.

1 onion, finely chopped
2 leeks (white part only), chopped
2 teaspoons olive oil
3 cups fish stock or 2 bottles
   (12 ounces each) clam juice
½ cup dry white wine
2 carrots, sliced
2 cloves garlic, minced
½ teaspoon fennel seed
½ teaspoon dried thyme

Salt and pepper, to taste
6 ounces crabmeat
6 ounces cooked small shrimp
¼ pound small scallops or
   red snapper fillet, cut in 1-inch
   pieces
¼ cup finely chopped Italian
   parsley
1 cup shredded Jarlsberg or
   Danish Emmenthal cheese

In a large soup kettle, sauté onion and leeks in oil until limp. Add the stock, wine, carrots, garlic, fennel seed, thyme, and salt and pepper, to taste. Cover and simmer 15 minutes. Add crab, shrimp, and scallops and simmer 3 to 5 minutes longer. Ladle into large bowls. Sprinkle with parsley and cheese. Makes 4 servings.

Brittany Fish Stew

Accompany this fast fish stew with garlic-coated crusty French bread and a light green salad.

1 medium onion, chopped
2 leeks (white part only), chopped
1 teaspoon olive oil
3 cups chicken stock
¾ cup dry white wine or vermouth
2 large potatoes, peeled and cut into ¼-inch slices

¼ teaspoon fennel seed
¼ teaspoon dried thyme
1 pound boneless red snapper or halibut
Salt and pepper, to taste
2 tablespoons chopped Italian parsley

In a large soup pot, sauté the onion and leeks in oil over medium heat, cooking until soft and glazed. Add the stock, wine, potatoes, fennel seed, and thyme. Bring to a boil, cover, and simmer until potatoes are tender, about 15 minutes. Cut the fish into 1-inch chunks and add to the soup. Cover and simmer 6 minutes longer or until fish flakes when prodded with a fork. Season with salt and pepper to taste. Ladle into large bowls and sprinkle with parsley. Makes 4 servings.

Spanish Fish Stew

Saffron and citrus peels enhance this fish stew with an intriguing flavor.

1 tablespoon olive oil
1 large onion, chopped
2 tomatoes, peeled, seeded, and
  chopped
½ cup dry white wine
4 cups fish stock
6 strands saffron
2 cloves garlic, minced
1 teaspoon grated lemon zest

1 teaspoon grated orange zest
3 tablespoons coarsely chopped
  parsley
1¼ pounds boneless firm white
  fish, such as monkfish, sword-
  fish, or rock fish, cut in chunks
8 mussels or small butter clams,
  cleaned
8 raw shrimp, in their shells

In a large skillet, heat the oil and sauté the onion until soft and glazed. Add the tomatoes and sauté for 2 to 3 minutes. Add wine and simmer briskly until reduced by one-third. Add the fish stock and boil until slightly reduced.

In a mortar, pound saffron, garlic, lemon peel, orange peel, and parsley together. Mix in a little of the hot stock and then return to the pan and boil briskly for 1 minute. Add fish, mussels, and shrimp to the pan. Cover and simmer just until fish barely flakes with a fork. Serve immediately in shallow soup bowls, ladling broth over each portion. Makes 4 servings.

Black Bean Soup

This hearty full-meal soup is refreshed with zestful condiments.

2 cups black beans
Water
1 pound ham shank, cut in large
  pieces
1 medium-sized onion, chopped
1 stalk celery with leaves, chopped
1 carrot, chopped
2 cloves garlic, minced
1 bay leaf
½ teaspoon dried oregano

¼ teaspoon ground cloves
1 small dried red pepper, seeds
  removed
½ cup dry red wine
1 can (8 ounces) tomato sauce
Salt and pepper, to taste
Yogurt or sour cream and chopped
  cilantro, for garnish
Lemon or lime wedges, for garnish

Place the beans in a large kettle. Add enough hot water to cover beans by 2 inches. Cover, bring to a boil, and boil 2 minutes. Remove from heat and let the beans soak, covered, for 1 hour; drain. Add 2 quarts of water to the beans, along with the ham shank, onion, celery, carrot, garlic, bay leaf, oregano, cloves, and pepper. Cover and simmer 1½ hours or until beans are almost tender. Add wine and tomato sauce and simmer 30 minutes longer. Discard bay leaf. Remove meat and chop it, discarding bones.

Spoon about one-third of the beans and some liquid into a blender or food processor and process until smooth. Return the purée to the soup and add the meat. Heat through and season with salt and pepper. Ladle into bowls, top each serving with a dollop of yogurt, and sprinkle with cilantro. Pass lemon wedges. Makes 6 servings.

Chicken and White Bean Soup

An aromatic chicken and vegetable soup makes a wonderful meal with a salad and crusty bread.

1 medium onion, diced
3 leeks, chopped (white part only)
1 teaspoon olive oil
2 cloves garlic, minced
4 cups chicken broth
4 chicken legs and thighs, skinned,
*   if desired*
1 tablespoon Dijon mustard

⅓ cup dry white wine
4 carrots, peeled and sliced
1 can (1 pound) white beans,
*   rinsed and drained*
2 tablespoons chopped parsley
1 teaspoon fresh thyme or
*   ¼ teaspoon dried thyme*
Salt and pepper, to taste

In a large soup pot, sauté the onion and leeks in oil over moderate heat. Add garlic, broth, chicken, mustard, and wine. Cover and simmer 40 minutes. Add carrots and beans and simmer 15 minutes longer or until chicken is tender. Add parsley, thyme, and salt and pepper, to taste. Remove the chicken from the pot, let cool slightly, and pull the meat from the bones. Skim fat from the broth, return the chicken to the soup, and heat through. Makes 6 servings.

Early California Soup

This is a colorful soup–stew for a full-meal dinner. Accompany it with crispy tortilla chips and a sliced orange and jicama salad.

1 onion, chopped
1 teaspoon olive oil
4 chicken legs and thighs, skinned,
   if desired
4 cups water
Few celery leaves, chopped
2 cloves garlic, minced
½ teaspoon cumin
½ teaspoon dried oregano
Salt and pepper, to taste
Small piece hot red pepper
   (optional)

1 ear corn, husked and cut in
   1-inch slices or cut kernels
   from cob
2 small yellow crookneck squash,
   sliced
2 small zucchini, sliced
¼ cup chopped cilantro
2 tablespoons roasted sunflower
   seeds
1 small avocado, peeled and diced
1 small red pepper, seeded and
   diced (optional)

In a large soup pot, sauté the onion in oil until soft. Add chicken, water, celery leaves, garlic, cumin, oregano, salt and pepper to taste, and hot pepper, if desired. Cover and simmer 45 minutes to 1 hour or until the chicken is tender. Lift chicken from broth and remove the meat from bones, tearing it into strips. Skim fat from broth. Bring to a boil and add the corn and squashes. Simmer 2 minutes or until vegetables are al dente. Add chicken and heat through. Ladle soup into bowls and sprinkle with cilantro and sunflower seeds. Scatter avocado pieces over the soup and garnish with red pepper, if desired. Makes 4 servings.

Savory Turkey and Vegetable Soup

Assorted vegetables, both roots and greens, enrich this healthy soup. It's a great way to use leftover roast turkey or chicken.

4 dried porcini or shiitake
*   mushrooms*
Water
4 cups chicken broth
2 leeks (white part only), sliced
2 carrots, sliced
2 turnips or parsnips, sliced
1½ tablespoons cornstarch blended
*   with 1½ tablespoons cold water*

½ bunch spinach, leaves only, cut
*   in ½-inch strips*
½ head butter lettuce, cut into
*   ½-inch strips*
3 cups cooked turkey or chicken,
*   pulled into strips*
2 tablespoons chopped parsley

Soak mushrooms in cold water for 15 minutes. Remove the mushrooms from the water and chop them, reserving the liquid. Bring chicken broth to a boil. Add the mushroom liquid, mushrooms, leeks, carrots, and turnips. Cover and simmer for 15 to 20 minutes or until vegetables are tender. Stir in cornstarch paste and cook until thickened. Add spinach, lettuce, and turkey and simmer until heated through. Ladle into large bowls and sprinkle with parsley. Makes 4 servings.

Note: If desired, add a splash of dry white wine for a special touch just before serving. If desired, simmer 2 skinned turkey drumsticks in the chicken broth for 1 hour at the beginning of the recipe, above. Remove and pull meat from the bones. Then continue with cooking the mushrooms and vegetables.

Lentil and Sausage Soup

A variety of sausages can flavor this wholesome soup.

2 cups small green lentils
1 medium sweet onion, chopped
1 celery stalk with leaves, chopped
1 carrot, peeled and chopped
8 sun-dried tomatoes, snipped
8 cups chicken or beef broth
2 cloves garlic, minced

1 cup chopped cooked ham
½ teaspoon dried thyme
1 bay leaf
¼ cup dry red wine
2 Polish sausages, summer
    sausages, or Italian sausages
Salt and pepper, to taste

Place the lentils, onion, celery, carrot, tomatoes, broth, garlic, ham, thyme, and bay leaf in a soup pot. Cover and simmer 45 minutes or until lentils are tender. Remove the bay leaf. Add the wine and sausages and simmer until sausages are cooked through, about 15 minutes longer. Remove sausages, slice them, and return to the pot. Season with salt and pepper to taste. Heat through. Makes 8 to 10 servings.

Moroccan Meatball Soup

Fresh chopped cilantro and juicy tomatoes enliven this spicy full-meal soup. It is a marvelous meal by itself especially when accompanied by a garlicky rosemary bread (see page 184) and a basket of pears or grapes.

1 onion, chopped
1 carrot, peeled and grated
1 stalk fennel or celery, chopped
2 teaspoons olive oil
5 cups beef broth
1 teaspoon grated fresh ginger root
½ teaspoon cumin
½ teaspoon freshly ground pepper

Salt, to taste
3 tablespoons tomato paste
Meatballs (recipe follows)
1 cup shredded Swiss chard leaves
   (optional)
2 Roma tomatoes, peeled and
   chopped
¼ cup chopped cilantro

In a large saucepan, sauté the onion, carrot, and fennel or celery in oil until soft. Add the broth, ginger, cumin, pepper, salt to taste, and tomato paste. Cover and simmer 25 minutes. Drop in meatballs and Swiss chard and cook 10 to 15 minutes longer. Add chopped tomatoes and cilantro just before serving. Makes 4 servings.

MEATBALLS:

1 pound ground turkey or lean
   ground lamb
3 tablespoons cornstarch
1 egg or 2 egg whites

3 tablespoons minced cilantro
1 clove garlic, chopped
½ teaspoon salt

In a bowl, combine the meatball ingredients and shape into ¾-inch balls.

Salads

A vinaigrette salad dressing, made in quantity, is a boon to the working cook. With ½ pint of dressing, already mixed in a slender shakeable jar in the refrigerator, it is easy to assemble a daily green salad in many styles. Wash the greens in advance and spin them dry, then store them in a plastic bag in the refrigerator, ready for tearing into bite-size pieces for salad making. The garnishes will vary with the season, using red and yellow cherry tomatoes, sprouts, mushrooms, jicama, cucumber, and such fruits as strawberries, Granny Smith apples, nectarines, pears, and cantaloupe or honeydew melon. Toasted pecans, walnuts, and filberts add a satisfying crunch to a green salad, and a sliver of blue cheese or Brie adds an elegant flourish.

Some salads make eye-catching entrées for warm weather dining. For these consider Papaya, Avocado, and Chicken Salad, Oriental Chicken and Fruit Salad, Crab-Stuffed Artichokes, or Smoked Salmon and Red Onions Casonova. With a crusty loaf of bread from a favorite bakery or the pantry and some frozen yogurt or ice cream, the stage is set for a satisfying meal.

Healthy Fruited Slaw

This refreshing salad is delicious for dinner. It is also excellent for lunch and packs easily in an insulated container for lunch at the office.

3 carrots, peeled
¼ head green cabbage
2 Granny Smith apples, cored and
    quartered
2 oranges, unpeeled and quartered
2 tablespoons parsley

1 tablespoon fresh oregano
4 tablespoons chutney
2 tablespoons red wine or
    raspberry vinegar
1 tablespoon sesame oil
2 teaspoons Dijon mustard

Fit the food processor with the shredder attachment and shred the carrots, cabbage, apples, oranges, parsley, and oregano. In a bowl, stir together the chutney, vinegar, oil, and mustard. Add slaw and mix to coat. Cover and chill. Use within two days. Makes about 1½ quarts.

Note: An optional way to handle the orange is to use a vegetable peeler to peel the zest. Then peel and discard the white peel and quarter the orange. For a different dressing omit chutney dressing and substitute Shallot Vinaigrette (see page 62).

Mushroom Fennel Salad

The bite of anise fennel, nutty cheese, and earthy mushrooms makes an intriguing salad combination.

½ pound mushrooms, thinly sliced
1 cup fennel, thinly sliced
¼ pound Gruyère or Jarlsberg
   cheese, cut in julienne strips
Mustard Vinaigrette (recipe
   follows)

Butter lettuce
1 cup cherry tomatoes
2 tablespoons chopped pistachios
2 tablespoons chopped parsley

In a bowl, combine the mushrooms, fennel, and cheese and pour the dressing over them. Cover and chill 1 hour, mixing once or twice. Spoon fennel mixture onto a platter or 4 plates lined with lettuce and surround with cherry tomatoes. Sprinkle with nuts and parsley. Makes 4 servings.

MUSTARD VINAIGRETTE:

¼ cup olive oil
2 tablespoons lemon juice
1 teaspoon Dijon mustard
½ teaspoon grated lemon zest

Salt and pepper, to taste
1 teaspoon chopped fresh tarragon
   or ¼ teaspoon dried tarragon

Place all of the dressing ingredients in a jar and cover tightly. Shake thoroughly to combine.

Spinach Platter Salad

This handsome vegetable salad might accompany a fish stew or grilled meats.

1 large bunch spinach, stems removed
¼ pound mushrooms, thinly sliced
1 small red pepper, seeded and diced
1 small red onion, halved and thinly sliced
½ cup alfalfa sprouts
2 stalks fennel
Parmesan Dressing (recipe follows)

Tear the spinach into bite-sized pieces and place on a large platter. Arrange the mushrooms, pepper, onion, sprouts, and fennel in rows on top. Drizzle with Parmesan Dressing. Makes 4 servings.

PARMESAN DRESSING:

¼ cup olive oil
1 tablespoon red wine vinegar
1 tablespoon lemon juice
Salt and pepper, to taste
1 clove garlic, minced
⅓ cup freshly grated Parmesan cheese

In a bowl or jar, whisk the dressing ingredients together.

Spicy Spinach Salad

A lively curry dressing uplifts a colorful spinach salad.

*1 bunch spinach, torn into
  bite-size pieces
1 cup halved cherry tomatoes
¼ pound button mushrooms, sliced*

*Curry Dressing (recipe follows)
2 tablespoons toasted sunflower
  seeds or pistachios*

In a bowl, combine the spinach, tomatoes, and mushrooms; pour the dressing over them and mix lightly. Scatter the sunflower seeds over the salad. Makes 4 servings.

CURRY DRESSING:

*2 tablespoons white wine vinegar
1 tablespoon dry white wine
1 teaspoon soy sauce
½ teaspoon dry mustard*

*¾ teaspoon curry powder
½ teaspoon sugar
¼ teaspoon freshly ground pepper
¼ cup canola or safflower oil*

In a bowl, combine the vinegar, wine, soy sauce, dry mustard, curry powder, sugar, and pepper. Whisk in the oil and chill dressing until ready to use.

Greens with Shallot Vinaigrette in Variation

Shallots lend a lively sweet bite to a vinaigrette for greens and fruit. Make the dressing in quantity ready to use spontaneously for a special salad. Vary the fruit embellishment to suit the season. Besides strawberries, red or green grapes, Bartlett or Comice pears, and Granny Smith or Fuji apples are other good choices.

½ cup olive oil
2 tablespoons Dijon mustard
3 tablespoons raspberry vinegar or
*   white wine vinegar*
¼ cup dry white wine
4 shallots, chopped (¼ cup)
1 teaspoon dried tarragon
Dash of salt and freshly ground
*   pepper*

Mixed greens: butter lettuce,
*   red oakleaf lettuce, arugula,*
*   mache (lamb's lettuce)*
Choice of fruit: strawberries,
*   grapes, pears, or apples*
Chopped pistachios or toasted
*   pecans*

SHALLOT VINAIGRETTE:

In a small bowl, stir together the oil and mustard to blend. Stir in the vinegar, wine, shallots, tarragon, salt, and pepper. Cover and chill until ready to use. If you prefer an emulsified dressing, blend the mixture in a blender or food processor. Makes 1 cup dressing or enough for about 12 servings.

Place desired greens in a bowl, add dressing, and mix to coat thoroughly. Spoon out on salad plates. Place fruit, diced if appropriate, on top of the greens and scatter the nuts over the salad.

Parsley Salad

This zestful salad, a specialty c? the Parisian restaurant Arpége, makes a delightful accompaniment to grilled fish.

2 cups chopped Italian parsley
¼ cup chopped arugula
2 tablespoons mixed chopped
* chives, tarragon, and thyme*

2 tablespoons extra virgin olive oil
1 teaspoon lemon juice
Salt and pepper, to taste

Place the parsley, arugula, chives, tarragon, and thyme in a bowl. Add the oil, lemon juice, and salt and pepper and mix lightly. Makes 2 servings.

Pico de Gallo

This Mexican salad, meaning the "rooster's beak," goes particularly well with grilled meats.

3 navel oranges, peeled and thinly sliced
1 small cucumber, peeled and thinly sliced
1 cup sliced jicama, cut in 1-inch strips
1 small red pepper, sliced in julienne strips

2 tablespoons olive oil
¼ cup orange juice
1 tablespoon white wine vinegar
Salt and cayenne, to taste
Chopped cilantro, for garnish

On a large plate, arrange the oranges, cucumber, jicama, and pepper in overlapping layers. Stir together the oil, orange juice, vinegar, and salt and cayenne to taste, and pour over the salad. Chill until serving time. Makes 4 servings.

Layered Gazpacho Salad

A spring-top, wide-mouth canning jar is an ideal container for holding this colorful salad as it marinates.

2 large tomatoes, peeled and
    thinly sliced
2 lemon cucumbers, peeled, thinly
    sliced
1 red or yellow bell pepper, seeded,
    julienned
¼ pound mushrooms, sliced

1 red onion, sliced
8 pitted oil-cured black olives
2 green onions, chopped
Salt and freshly ground black
    pepper, to taste
Garlic Basil Vinaigrette (recipe
    follows)

In a large wide-mouth jar or bowl, alternate layers of tomatoes, cucumbers, pepper, mushrooms, and onion. Sprinkle each layer with salt and pepper and top with olives and onions, placed in circles. Pour the Garlic Basil Vinaigrette over the salad. Cover and refrigerate at least 1 hour. Makes 4 servings.

GARLIC BASIL VINAIGRETTE:

¼ cup olive oil
1½ tablespoons tarragon-flavored
    white wine vinegar
1½ tablespoons dry white wine

1 tablespoon chopped fresh basil or
    ¾ teaspoon dried basil
Salt and pepper, to taste

Mix the Vinaigrette ingredients together in either a bowl or a jar.

Shrimp and Grape Leaf Salad Plate

With Stuffed Grape Leaves on hand, this salad plate goes together in a jiffy.

Oakleaf or butter lettuce
6 Stuffed Grape Leaves (see
    page 249)
6 jumbo cooked shrimp, shelled,
    with tails on
6 cherry tomatoes

1 small lemon cucumber, peeled
    and sliced
2 ounces feta cheese
6 Nicoise-style olives
2 lemon wedges

Line 2 dinner-size plates with lettuce. Arrange in clusters the Stuffed Grape Leaves, shrimp, tomatoes, cucumber slices, a chunk of cheese, and olives. Garnish with lemon wedges. Makes 2 servings.

Lemon Grass Tabbouleh with Shrimp and Grapes

Lemon grass and cilantro lend an intriguing flavor to couscous for a salad entrée.

½ cup couscous
¾ cup boiling water
¾ cup cilantro sprigs
2 cloves garlic, minced
3 tablespoons pistachios
1 tablespoon chopped lemon grass
2 tablespoons olive oil

1 tablespoon lime or lemon juice
Assorted greens: butter lettuce,
    red oakleaf lettuce, radicchio
½ pound small cooked shrimp or
    crabmeat
1 cup seedless grapes
Cilantro, for garnish

Place the couscous in a bowl and pour the water over it. Cover and let stand 10 minutes. Cool to room temperature. Place the cilantro, garlic, pistachios, lemon grass, olive oil, and lime juice in a blender container and purée until finely minced. Add to couscous and mix lightly with a fork to separate grains.

Line 2 plates with lettuce. Spoon the tabbouleh into a mound on each plate and surround it with seafood and grapes; then garnish with cilantro. Makes 2 servings.

Crab-Stuffed Artichokes

Big plump artichokes stuffed with seafood make a regal light supper.

2 large artichokes, cooked and
 chilled
Butter lettuce or assorted greens
½ pound crabmeat, imitation
 crabmeat, or small cooked
 shrimp

Yogurt–Herb Dressing (recipe
 follows)
6 to 8 cherry tomatoes
2 hard-cooked eggs, cut in wedges
 (optional)
Mediterranean-style olives, for
 garnish

Pull out the center leaves of the artichokes and scoop out the chokes.
Arrange the lettuce leaves on individual dinner-size plates and place an
artichoke on each bed of greens. Spoon dressing in the center of each
artichoke and top with seafood. Surround the artichokes with tomatoes,
eggs, and olives. Makes 2 servings.

YOGURT–HERB DRESSING:

2 tablespoons plain yogurt
2 tablespoons sour cream
½ teaspoon fresh lemon juice
½ teaspoon Dijon or Parisian
 mustard

1 tablespoon minced parsley
2 teaspoons minced chives or green
 onion tops

In a bowl, combine the yogurt, sour cream, lemon juice, and mustard.
Blend in the parsley and chives.

Smoked Salmon and Red Onions Casonova

This decorative salad plate is a specialty of a charming Carmel, California café. Accompany it with a crusty whole-grain bread.

2 tablespoons olive oil
1 tablespoon lemon juice
1 tablespoon white wine vinegar
1/2 teaspoon Dijon mustard
1/4 cup freshly shredded Parmesan
    cheese
Salt and pepper, to taste
3 cups mixed salad greens
    (radicchio, mache, oakleaf
    lettuce, and chicory)

1/8 pound mushrooms, thinly sliced
6 ounces thinly sliced smoked
    salmon
1 small red onion, sliced and
    separated into rings
2 tablespoons chopped parsley or
    chives

In a bowl, stir together the oil, lemon juice, vinegar, mustard, cheese, and salt and pepper. Add the greens and mushrooms and mix lightly. Spoon the salad onto 2 dinner-size places. Cut the salmon into 2-inch strips and drape it over the greens. Scatter onion rings over the salmon. Sprinkle with parsley or chives. Makes 2 servings.

Green Bean, Mushroom, and Seafood Salad

A choice of seafood can embellish this fresh-tasting full-meal salad.

½ pound green beans, French-cut
¼ pound mushrooms, sliced
1 shallot, chopped
¼ cup diced jicama (optional)
2 tablespoons olive oil
2 tablespoons white wine vinegar
1 teaspoon fresh chopped tarragon
    or ¼ teaspoon dried tarragon

1 teaspoon Dijon mustard
Salt and pepper, to taste
Salad greens
½ pound cooked scallops, mussels,
    or medium shrimp
2 tablespoons chopped parsley or
    chives

Cook the beans in boiling salted water to cover for 5 to 7 minutes or until crisp tender. Drain and rinse under cold running water. Place them in a bowl and add the mushrooms, shallots, and jicama. Mix together the oil, vinegar, tarragon, mustard, and salt and pepper to taste. Pour over the vegetables and mix lightly. Arrange greens on 2 plates, top with the vegetable medley, and surround it with seafood. Sprinkle with parsley. Makes 2 servings.

Crab and Citrus Salad Vinaigrette

A pinwheel of grapefruit, oranges, and avocado makes a picture-perfect salad plate for centering with crabmeat. Imitation crab (surimi) makes an economical choice.

Butter lettuce
1 pink grapefruit, peeled and
    sectioned
2 navel oranges or blood oranges,
    peeled and sliced or sectioned
1 small avocado, sliced
½ pound cooked crabmeat
3 tablespoons safflower oil
1 tablespoon lemon juice

1 tablespoon white wine vinegar
½ teaspoon freshly grated lemon
    zest
½ teaspoon Dijon mustard
1 shallot, chopped
Salt and pepper to taste
2 tablespoons pistachios or toasted
    slivered almonds

Line 2 dinner-size plates with a bed of butter lettuce. Arrange the grapefruit, oranges, and avocado in a pinwheel design. Spoon the crabmeat in the center. Mix together the oil, lemon juice, vinegar, lemon zest, mustard, shallot, and salt and pepper and spoon over the salad just before serving. Sprinkle with nuts. Makes 2 servings.

Oriental Chicken and Fruit Salad

Kiwi fruit and sliced oranges make a refreshing counterpoint to this chicken salad.

2 split cooked chicken breasts
Sesame Soy Dressing (recipe
    follows)
Butter lettuce or mixed salad greens
2 navel oranges, thinly sliced

2 kiwi fruit, peeled and thinly
    sliced
½ cup strawberries, hulled
2 tablespoons toasted slivered
    almonds or pistachios

Skin and bone the chicken and tear the meat into strips. Place in a bowl and toss with half the dressing. Arrange lettuce on 2 plates and make semi-circle of oranges and kiwi fruit on each plate. Scatter chicken and berries over the fruit. Drizzle with remaining dressing. Makes 2 servings.

SESAME SOY DRESSING:

2 tablespoons safflower oil
1 tablespoon soy sauce
1 tablespoon sesame oil
1 tablespoon lemon juice
2 teaspoons honey

½ teaspoon freshly grated lemon
    zest
Dash of liquid hot pepper
    seasoning (optional)

In a bowl, combine all of the dressing ingredients.

Papaya, Avocado, and Chicken Salad

Papaya and avocado are natural partners in a salad plate with grilled chicken strips. For a variation substitute seafood or roast pork.

2 split chicken breasts, boned
1 tablespoon olive oil
1 tablespoon lemon juice
Salt and pepper, to taste
3 cups mixed salad greens

Lemon Tarragon Dressing (recipe follows)
1 small papaya, halved, seeded, and sliced
1 small avocado, peeled and sliced

Drizzle chicken breasts with oil and lemon juice and season with salt and pepper to taste. Grill or broil until cooked through, turning, allowing about 4 minutes on a side. Slice chicken into strips. Meanwhile, toss salad greens with dressing and arrange on 2 dinner-size plates. Top with papaya and avocado slices. Arrange warm chicken strips over all. Makes 2 servings.

LEMON TARRAGON DRESSING:

2 tablespoons safflower oil or olive oil
1 tablespoon lemon juice
1 tablespoon white wine vinegar
½ teaspoon grated lemon zest

¼ teaspoon Dijon mustard
1 teaspoon chopped fresh tarragon or ¼ teaspoon dried tarragon
Salt and pepper, to taste

Combine the dressing ingredients in a small bowl.

Variation: Instead of the warm chicken strips, substitute ½ pound cooked shrimp or surimi crabmeat or roast pork, cut into strips.

Fruited Blue Cheese Salad Plate

Consider this colorful salad for a festive combination salad-cheese course.

2 tablespoons olive oil
1 teaspoon Dijon mustard
1 tablespoon raspberry vinegar
1 tablespoon dry white wine
1 shallot, chopped
½ teaspoon dried tarragon
Salt and freshly ground pepper, to
    taste

2 cups mixed greens: butter
    lettuce, red oakleaf lettuce,
    arugula, mache
1 Granny Smith or Fuji apple,
    halved, cored, and sliced
½ cup red seedless grapes
2 ounces blue cheese
2 tablespoons chopped pistachios or
    toasted pecans

In a small bowl, stir together the oil and mustard to blend. Stir in vinegar, wine, shallots, tarragon, and salt and pepper. Place greens in a bowl, add dressing, and mix to coat thoroughly. Spoon the greens on 2 salad plates. Arrange apples, grapes, and cheese on top of the greens and sprinkle with nuts. Makes 2 servings.

   Note: As an option, tarragon white wine vinegar or sherry vinegar may replace the raspberry vinegar.

Gingered Fruit and Feta Salad

Ginger sparks this refreshing mixed fruit and cheese salad.

Ginger Dressing (recipe follows)
3 cups assorted salad greens
   (butter lettuce, mache,
   radicchio, and oakleaf lettuces)
1½ cups seedless red and green
   grapes

2 kiwi fruit, peeled and sliced
1 cup strawberries, hulled and
   halved
2 oranges, sectioned
2 ounces feta cheese crumbs

Pour half of the dressing over the greens and mix lightly. Arrange on a large platter or individual salad plates. Place the grapes, kiwi fruit, strawberries, and oranges in a bowl and pour the remaining dressing over them, mixing lightly. Spoon the fruit on top of the greens and sprinkle with cheese. Makes 4 servings.

GINGER DRESSING:

¼ cup orange juice
1 tablespoon canola oil
1 tablespoon lemon juice
1 tablespoon Dijon mustard

2 teaspoons grated ginger root
½ teaspoon orange zest
½ teaspoon lemon zest

Mix together the dressing ingredients in a small bowl.

Mediterranean Fruit Salad

Mint stimulates this fruit salad for a tasteful finish to a barbecue meal.

2 navel oranges, peeled and sliced
¾ cup red seedless grapes
¾ cup green seedless grapes
1 small red onion, thinly sliced
3 tablespoons olive oil
1½ tablespoons lemon juice

Salt and pepper, to taste
1 tablespoon finely chopped mint
Curly endive or watercress
½ cup feta cheese, broken into
    chunks
3 tablespoons pistachios

Place the oranges, grapes, and onion in a bowl. Stir together the oil, lemon juice, salt and pepper, and mint; spoon over the fruit and mix gently. Arrange endive on 4 individual plates. Arrange the fruit mixture on the endive and sprinkle with cheese and nuts. Makes 4 servings.

Pizza, Pasta, and Egg Dishes

Flour tortillas and pita breads come in handy for the working cook as instant bases for individual pizzas. Flour tortillas make plate-size cartwheels for Pizza Monterey, Tortilla Flats, or Armenian Pizzas. Whole wheat pita breads form a pocket for Greek Pitas and a disk for Prosciutto and Pear Pita Pizzas.

Pasta is a jewel since it cooks quickly. Consider either fresh pasta or high-quality dried pasta for turning out a fast, filling supper.

Omelets are an ideal spontaneous dish, taking only minutes to whisk, cook, fold, and turn out. Frittatas are another option, using eggs and fresh vegetables that are generally on hand in such combinations as Cherry Tomato and Spinach Frittata or Mushroom and Prosciutto Frittata. For a dramatic showpiece for a weekend brunch, the Dutch Babie with Raspberries and Orange Cream turns out golden brown and puffy, a stylish centerpiece and a savory delight.

Pizza Monterey

Flavors of the Monterey Bay Peninsula inspire this fast, hot tortilla pizza.

2 8-inch flour tortillas
1 cup shredded Monterey Jack
   cheese
¼ pound small cooked shrimp or
   surimi crabmeat

1 jar (6 ounces) marinated
   artichoke hearts, drained
8 cherry tomatoes, halved
2 tablespoons chopped fresh basil
3 tablespoons shredded Parmesan
   cheese

Lay out tortillas on a baking sheet. Sprinkle with Monterey Jack cheese and bake in a preheated 425° oven for 5 minutes or until slightly crispy. Scatter the shrimp on the top of the tortillas. Then arrange artichoke hearts and cherry tomatoes, cut side down, on top. Sprinkle with basil and Parmesan cheese. Return to the oven for 4 to 5 minutes or until heated through. Makes 2 servings.

Armenian Pizzas

Flour tortillas make a neat pizza base for plate-size spicy lamb pizzas.

*¾ pound ground lamb or ground
   turkey*
*Salt and freshly ground pepper, to
   taste*
1 clove garlic, minced
¼ teaspoon ground allspice
¼ teaspoon cumin
1 shallot or 2 green onions, chopped

⅛ pound mushrooms, sliced
*2 tablespoons pistachios or pine
   nuts*
¼ cup tomato sauce
1 egg white
¾ cup grated Monterey Jack cheese
2 (9- or 10-inch) flour tortillas

In a bowl, mix together the lamb, salt, pepper, garlic, allspice, cumin, shallot, mushrooms, pistachios, tomato sauce, and egg white. Lay each tortilla on a baking sheet and pat half of the meat mixture on each one, covering to within 1 inch of the edge. Sprinkle with cheese. Bake in a preheated 425° oven for 10 to 12 minutes or until meat is browned and the edges are crisp. Makes 2 servings.

Prosciutto and Pear Pizzas

Whole wheat pita breads make neat, wholesome pizza bases for this fruit and ham supper sandwich.

2 whole wheat pita breads
1 large Bosc or Anjou pear
2 ounces thinly sliced prosciutto
8 soft sun-dried tomatoes, snipped

1 cup (4 ounces) shredded
    Jarlsberg cheese
2 tablespoons pistachios or pine
    nuts

Lay out pita breads on a baking pan. Halve, core, and slice pears and arrange each half in a fan on top of each bread. Top with prosciutto strips and scatter tomatoes, cheese, and nuts over the prosciutto. Bake in a pre-heated 450° oven for 10 minutes or until cheese is melted and breads are crispy. Makes 2 servings.

Seafood Quesadillas

Hot grilled flour tortillas provide a sandwich for seafood and cheese. This variation of a Southwestern food makes a great snack to top with avocado and sour cream.

4 (6-inch) flour tortillas
½ cup (2 ounces) grated Monterey
   Jack cheese
½ cup (2 ounces) grated cheddar
   cheese
1 green onion, chopped

¼ pound scallops, cut in half
   horizontally
¼ pound crabmeat
4 cherry tomatoes, halved
1 small avocado
Sour cream or yogurt, for topping

Place 2 tortillas on a baking sheet or a cutting board and sprinkle with both cheeses. Scatter onion over the cheeses and arrange seafood on top, leaving a ½-inch border around the edge. Cover with a tortilla, transfer to a hot skillet, and grill, turning to barely brown both sides. Cook until heated through and the cheese is melted. Transfer to plates and top with tomato halves. Peel and slice the avocado and make a pinwheel on top. Dollop with sour cream or yogurt. Makes 2 servings.

Tortilla Flats

Plate-size flour tortillas form a neat base for individual pizzas. Vary the toppings to suit your whim.

1 tablespoon olive oil
3 green onions, chopped
*1 small zucchini, ends trimmed
   and thinly sliced*
¼ pound mushrooms, sliced
1 clove garlic, minced
*6 slices salami or 3 ounces
   prosciutto, julienned*
6 soft sun-dried tomatoes, diced

2 (8-inch) flour tortillas
*2 tablespoons tomato paste or
   spaghetti sauce*
*2 teaspoons fresh chopped oregano
   or ½ teaspoon dried oregano*
*½ cup shredded Monterey Jack
   cheese*
*2 tablespoons grated Romano
   cheese*

Heat oil in a skillet over medium-high heat and sauté the onion, zucchini, mushrooms, and garlic until glazed, about 2 to 3 minutes. Add the salami and tomatoes and set aside. Place tortillas on a baking sheet and spread each with tomato paste. Sprinkle with oregano. Divide vegetable mixture evenly over each tortilla and sprinkle with the cheeses. Bake in a preheated 400° oven for 6 to 8 minutes or until cheese is melted and tortilla edges are lightly browned. Makes 2 servings.

Brittany Galettes
with Ham and Cheese

Buckwheat traditionally flavors the plate-size crêpes which are popular in Brittany. Fillings can vary with the fancy of the cook.

2 eggs
1½ cups milk
1 cup buckwheat pancake mix
2 tablespoons canola oil
Butter for frying

8 slices ham, cut in 4 by 6-inch
*   rectangles*
8 slices Gruyère or Jarlsberg cheese
*   (about 4 ounces), cut in*
*   4 by 6-inch rectangles*

Place the eggs, milk, pancake mix, and oil in a blender or food processor fitted with a steel blade and blend until smooth. Heat a large skillet or griddle, about 12 inches in diameter, and add 1½ teaspoons of butter. When the butter stops sizzling, pour in about ¼ cup batter and tilt pan to coat surface. Cook until golden brown underneath and remove from pan, cooking only one side. Repeat with remaining batter, stacking galettes (crêpes) as they are finished. If desired, cover and refrigerate until ready to fill.

   To fill, place a slice of ham and cheese on the unbrowned side of each pancake. Fold over the opposite sides like an envelope. Place on a lightly buttered baking sheet and heat in a preheated 400° oven for 5 minutes or until heated through. Makes 8 galettes or about 4 servings.

Greek Pitas

With the meat sauce on hand, these pocket breads make a fast meal.

*1 pint Greek Meat Sauce
    (see page 132)*
2 pita breads
*½ cup shredded Monterey Jack or
    Jarlsberg cheese*

*2 tablespoons chopped pistachios
    or pine nuts*
1 Roma tomato, sliced
2 green onions, chopped
Handful of sprouts

Place meat sauce in a greased casserole and heat in a preheated 350° oven for 20 minutes or until heated through. Wrap pita breads in foil and heat in the oven alongside the sauce for the last 10 minutes of baking time. Split breads in half for open sandwiches or cut crosswise in half to spoon fillings into the pocket. Top or fill breads with the meat sauce, cheese, nuts, tomato, onions, and sprouts. Makes 2 servings.

Vegetable Pita Pockets

A variety of vegetable fillings can enhance wholesome whole wheat pita breads.

4 whole wheat pita breads
¼ pound Jarlsberg, Muenster, or Monterey Jack cheese (low-fat cheese, if desired), thinly sliced
¼ pound mushrooms, sliced
1 small avocado, peeled and sliced

12 cherry tomatoes, halved
1 cup alfalfa sprouts
2 green onions, chopped
¼ cup plain yogurt
3 tablespoons roasted sunflower seeds

Slit open 1 side of the pita breads. Wrap breads in foil and bake them in a preheated 350° oven for 10 minutes or until heated through. Fill each bread with cheese, mushrooms, avocado slices, tomatoes, sprouts, onions, yogurt, and sunflower seeds. Makes 4 servings.

Angel Hair Pasta with Clams

If choice whole clams or steamed mussels are available, this is a quick-to-prepare entrée. Canned clams may also be used.

½ pound whole cooked clams or
   mussels
½ cup clam juice, or fish or
   chicken stock
2 tablespoons olive oil
4 shallots, chopped
2 cloves garlic, minced
¼ cup vermouth

¼ cup heavy cream
2 tablespoons chopped fresh basil
2 tablespoons chopped fresh parsley
Salt and freshly ground pepper
½ pound angel hair pasta
⅓ cup freshly grated Parmesan
   cheese
Basil sprigs, for garnish

Use fresh cooked clams or choice canned whole clams; reserve juice. In a large skillet, heat oil and sauté the shallots and garlic until soft. Add clam juice and vermouth and reduce by half. Add cream and reduce slightly. Add clams and heat through. Season with basil, parsley, and salt and pepper to taste. In a large pot, cook the pasta in boiling salted water until al dente. Drain pasta thoroughly, transfer to a bowl, and toss with the sauce. Serve with grated cheese sprinkled over the pasta and garnish with a few basil sprigs. Makes 2 servings.

Angel Hair Pasta
with Smoked Salmon and Basil

This fresh herb and seafood sauce goes together in a jiffy for an elegant pasta first course or entrée.

¼ pound smoked salmon, diced	3 tablespoons chopped pistachios
¼ cup chopped fresh basil	Salt and pepper, to taste
¼ cup chopped Italian parsley	3 tablespoons virgin olive oil
1 clove garlic, minced	½ pound angel hair pasta

In a bowl, combine the salmon, basil, parsley, garlic, pistachios, salt and pepper, and 1 tablespoon oil. Cook pasta in boiling salted water until al dente; drain thoroughly. Toss the pasta with the remaining oil and spoon onto warm plates or shallow soup bowls. Spoon the salmon-basil sauce on top. Makes 2 generous servings.

Pasta with Pesto Primavera

Pesto gives an uplift to this wholesome vegetable-laced pasta dish.

1 tablespoon olive oil
*1 small zucchini, ends trimmed,
   julienned*
*1 yellow squash, ends trimmed,
   julienned*
2 green onions, chopped
*1 dozen sugar snap peas or pea
   pods, trimmed*
1 tablespoon butter

*2 tablespoons pine nuts or
   pistachios*
¼ cup whipping cream
8 cherry tomatoes, halved
*2 tablespoons Pesto Sauce
   (see page 243)*
*½ pound fresh fettuccine or
   tagliarini*
*3 tablespoons freshly grated
   Romano cheese*

Heat oil in a large skillet over medium-high heat and sauté julienned squashes, onions, and sugar snaps until glazed, about 2 minutes. Push the vegetables to the side of the pan. Add butter and nuts and sauté until lightly browned. Add the cream, tomatoes, and Pesto Sauce and heat through. Meanwhile, cook fettuccine in a large pot of boiling salted water until al dente, about 3 minutes; drain well and place in a warm serving bowl. Spoon hot vegetables over pasta, mix lightly and spoon onto dinner plates. Sprinkle with cheese. Makes 2 servings.

Spaghetti with Browned Butter and Meat Sauce

Browned butter adds a special excitement to everyday spaghetti and meat sauce.

6 ounces spaghetti
1 pint Greek Meat Sauce
  (see page 132)

2 tablespoons butter
⅓ cup grated Parmesan or
  Romano cheese

Cook spaghetti in boiling salted water for 10 minutes or until al dente; drain. Meanwhile, heat meat sauce in a saucepan or microwave until hot through. Heat butter until bubbly and slightly browned and pour over spaghetti; mix lightly. Spoon spaghetti onto plates, top with meat sauce, and sprinkle with cheese. Makes 2 servings.

Asparagus and Eggs Italian-Style

When fresh asparagus is in season, this makes a fast, tasty treat.

¾ pound asparagus
1 tablespoon butter or margarine
2 eggs
Salt and freshly ground pepper, to
    taste

3 ounces thinly sliced prosciutto or
    ham, in strips
¼ cup shredded Parmesan or
    Romano cheese

Trim the ends from the asparagus and cook in boiling salted water until tender, about 5 to 7 minutes; drain. Divide the butter between two individual ramekins (casseroles) and melt in a preheated 350° oven. Break an egg into each ramekin, sprinkle with salt and pepper, and bake in the oven until whites are just barely set, about 7 minutes. Arrange asparagus and prosciutto alongside each egg, sprinkle with cheese, and continue baking until cheese melts, about 2 minutes longer. Makes 2 servings.

Note: If desired, ¼ pound small cooked shrimp can replace the prosciutto.

Swiss Potato Omelet

This hearty brunch or supper dish goes together in a jiffy with cooked potatoes on hand.

2 medium boiling potatoes
1 tablespoon olive oil or butter
2 shallots or green onions, chopped
½ cup diced cooked ham
4 eggs

1 tablespoon milk or half-and-half
2 tablespoons chopped parsley
Salt and pepper, to taste
½ cup (2 ounces) shredded
    Gruyère or Jarlsberg cheese

Cook whole, unpeeled potatoes in boiling salted water until barely tender, about 15 to 20 minutes; drain well. Peel and slice potatoes ¼ inch thick. Melt the oil in a large skillet with an ovenproof handle. Add shallots and sauté until soft. Add ham and sliced potatoes and sauté until lightly browned. Whisk eggs in a bowl with milk, parsley, and salt and pepper. Pour egg mixture over potato mixture. Cook until set. Shake skillet, occasionally slipping a spatula around edge to allow egg mixture to run underneath. Sprinkle cheese on top and slip under the broiler to melt cheese. Makes 2 generous servings.

Smoked Salmon Omelet

Smoked salmon and Yogurt Cheese give an elegant touch to the classic omelet for a swift entrée.

4 eggs
Salt and pepper, to taste
2 teaspoons butter
2 slices smoked salmon or lox

¼ cup Yogurt Cheese
   (see page 248) or sour cream
Minced chives or parsley, for
   garnish

For each omelet, whisk together 2 eggs and salt and pepper. Heat an 8-inch omelet pan, add 1 teaspoon of the butter, and when it stops foaming add beaten eggs all at once. Slip a thin spatula under the eggs just as soon as they set and lift to let the uncooked eggs flow underneath. When set, but still creamy on top, lay 1 slice of salmon across the omelet, top with a dollop of Yogurt Cheese, fold over, and turn out of the pan. Sprinkle with chives. Repeat with remaining omelet. Makes 2 servings.

Cherry Tomato and Spinach Frittata

Scarlet cherry tomato discs dot this bright green spinach frittata that cuts into neat pie-shaped wedges.

1 bunch green onions, chopped
1 teaspoon olive oil
1 bunch fresh spinach, stems
* removed*
½ cup plain yogurt or Yogurt
* Cheese (see page 248)*
2 eggs

Dash of salt and pepper
2 teaspoons chopped fresh tarragon
* or ½ teaspoon dried tarragon*
¼ cup shredded Parmesan or
* Romano cheese*
8 cherry tomatoes, halved
Yogurt, for accompaniment

In a large skillet, sauté the onions in oil until limp. Add the spinach and cook 1 minute, uncovered, until barely limp. Turn into a blender container or food processor fitted with a steel blade and add the yogurt, eggs, salt and pepper, tarragon, and half of the cheese. Blend until finely minced. Turn into a lightly oiled 9-inch pie pan and arrange cherry tomatoes, cut side down, on top. Sprinkle with remaining cheese. Bake in a preheated 350° oven for 30 minutes or until set. Cut into wedges and serve each portion with a spoonful of yogurt. Makes 6 servings.

Leek and Prosciutto Frittata

Sautéed leeks and ribbons of prosciutto lace an easy egg dish for a supper entrée or brunch dish.

3 leeks (white part only), thinly
   sliced
2 teaspoons olive oil
4 eggs
Salt and pepper, to taste
½ teaspoon dried tarragon

3 tablespoons chopped parsley
4 ounces thinly sliced prosciutto or
   ham
¼ cup freshly shredded Romano
   or Parmesan cheese

Using a large non-stick skillet, sauté the leeks in 1 teaspoon of the oil until soft and glazed. Add remaining teaspoon of oil to the pan. Beat the eggs until blended and mix in salt, pepper, tarragon, parsley, and half the prosciutto and cheese. Pour in egg mixture and cook over medium-high heat without stirring until the edges are lightly browned. Sprinkle with remaining prosciutto and cheese. Slip the skillet under the broiler to brown the top lightly. Cut into wedges to serve. Makes 2 generous servings.

Mushroom and Prosciutto Frittata

This quick 10-minute entrée needs only a salad and crusty bread for accompaniment. It makes a fun brunch dish as well.

1 tablespoon unsalted butter
2 shallots, chopped
1 ounce prosciutto, slivered
¼ pound mushrooms, sliced
4 eggs

Dash pepper
2 tablespoons grated Parmesan or
   Romano cheese
2 tablespoons chopped Italian
   parsley

Melt the butter in a 10-inch oven-proof skillet. Add shallots and prosciutto and cook over medium heat until shallots are golden. Add mushrooms and cook 1 minute. Beat the eggs with pepper, cheese, and parsley and pour into the skillet. Lower heat slightly and cook just until the bottom is set. Place the skillet under the broiler and cook until slightly puffed and set, about 1 to 2 minutes. Makes 2 servings.

Dutch Babie with Raspberries and Orange Cream

This puffy pancake has a topping of orange-flavored sour cream and fresh berries.

3 eggs
1 cup milk
1 tablespoon honey plus 1 teaspoon honey
1 teaspoon grated orange zest
¾ cup all-purpose flour

¼ cup plain yogurt
¼ cup sour cream
3 tablespoons undiluted orange juice concentrate
1 pint raspberries or strawberries, hulled and halved

Combine the eggs, milk, 1 tablespoon honey, orange peel, and flour in a blender or food processor fitted with a steel blade. Purée until smooth. Spray a 9-inch round baking dish with vegetable cooking spray and pour in the batter. Bake in a preheated 425° oven for 20 minutes or until puffed and golden brown. Meanwhile, stir together the yogurt, sour cream, orange juice concentrate, and 1 teaspoon honey and turn into a serving container. Spoon berries into a bowl. Serve hot pancake with berries and Orange Cream spooned over the top. Makes 4 servings.

Note: Blueberries or blackberries may be substituted for the above berries or garnish with sliced nectarines or peaches.

Baked Mushrooms with Chèvre

This fast entrée with fresh mushrooms is excellent with a salad for a light dinner.

⅓ pound large white or shiitake mushrooms, about 2 to 2½ inches in diameter
2 tablespoons butter
3 tablespoons chopped parsley
1 clove garlic, minced

½ teaspoon chopped fresh tarragon or ⅛ teaspoon dried tarragon
2 ounces chèvre
1 ounce prosciutto or ham, thinly sliced

Separate the mushroom stems from the caps and chop the stems. Slice each cap into 4 or 5 slices, keeping the slices together so that they retain the shape of the whole mushroom. Arrange the caps in small baking dishes and tuck the chopped stems on top of each. Melt the butter and mix in the parsley, garlic, and tarragon. Drizzle the butter mixture over the mushrooms. Bake in a preheated 425° oven for 5 minutes. Arrange a slice of cheese and prosciutto on top of each dish and continue baking for 5 minutes longer or until cheese melts. Makes 2 servings.

Entrées:
Fish, Poultry,
and Meat

The entrées included here offer countless options for the working cook. Barbecue dishes lend themselves to overnight marinating, ready for quick grilling the next day.

Some larger cuts of meat, fish, and poultry are ideal to oven-bake for one meal and use in a salad or sandwich the next day. Far Eastern London Broil, Butterflied Lamb, Lemon and Herb-Basted Turkey Breast, and Baked Salmon with Pistachio Aioli fill this dual need.

The cook who packs and totes a lunch cherishes entrées yielding wholesome meats that are appetizing cold the following day. Gingered Turkey Patties, Sprouted Lamb Loaves, Greek Sausages, and sliceable terrines or loaves such as Smoked Almond Turkey Terrine, Veal Loaf Cordon Bleu, and Pistachio-Studded Chicken Terrine are excellent a day or two later.

Add some whimsy to the dinner table with a sealed package on a plate at each place setting. Open the steaming contents to find Lamb Bandit Style or Sausages and Spuds in a Bag. Either one is easy to assemble and novel to serve.

Stir-fries present a handsome complete entrée plate and go together in a jiffy. Baked and broiled fish streamline the dinner preparations with their fast cooking technique.

Oriental Baked Trout

Whole trout are a snap to bake, and here they take on zestful lime and ginger seasonings.

Lime – Ginger Marinade
(recipe follows)
2 (1 to 1½ pound) whole trout

Cilantro or watercress, for garnish
1 lime, cut in wedges

Place trout in a glass baking dish, spoon the Lime–Ginger Marinade inside the cavity, and refrigerate for 30 minutes. Bake in a 450° oven for 10 minutes per inch of thickness. Peel off the skin and fillet fish. Arrange on 4 plates, tuck in cilantro, and garnish with lime wedges. Makes 4 servings.

LIME – GINGER MARINADE:

2 tablespoons dry sherry
1½ teaspoons light soy sauce
1 tablespoon lime juice

1 teaspoon grated ginger root
1 green onion, chopped

Combine the marinade ingredients.

Capered Turbot in a Vegetable Cloak

A melange of sautéed fresh vegetables smothers quickly-broiled fish.

¾ pound turbot or sole fillets
Salt and pepper, to taste
2 teaspoons lemon juice
2 teaspoons olive oil, plus
    1 tablespoon olive oil
¼ pound mushrooms, thinly sliced
2 green onions, chopped

1 medium tomato, peeled, seeded,
    and diced
1 clove garlic, minced
2 tablespoons chopped parsley
1 teaspoon capers
1 tablespoon chopped fresh basil or
    ¾ teaspoon dried basil

Place fish fillets on a broiling pan. Season with salt and pepper and sprinkle with mixture of lemon juice and 2 teaspoons of olive oil. Using a large skillet heat the 1 tablespoon oil and sauté the mushrooms, onions, tomato, and garlic for about 1 minute, or until heated through. Add the parsley, capers, and basil; stir and remove from heat. Broil the fish until golden brown, about 4 minutes (it is not necessary to turn it). Transfer fish to individual plates and cover with sautéed vegetables. Makes 2 servings.

Leek and Snapper Packets

Either foil or parchment can encase neat packets of ginger-spiced leeks and fish. Assemble this entrée in advance, ready for last minute baking.

2 leeks
1 teaspoon olive oil
1½ teaspoons finely chopped
  ginger root
⅓ cup dry white wine
1 teaspoon grated lemon peel

2 (6-ounce) snapper or salmon
  fillets
Salt and pepper, to taste
4 lemon slices
4 sprigs parsley

Cut the green tops off the leeks and trim the root ends. Split white portion lengthwise and wash thoroughly under cold running water. Drain. Cut into 1¼-inch julienne matchstick pieces. In a large skillet, heat the oil over moderate heat, add leeks and ginger root and sauté, stirring, until soft. Add the wine and lemon peel and cook down until reduced to a glaze.

Have ready two sheets of aluminum foil or parchment paper, each 11 inches square. Divide the leek mixture equally in the center of each piece of foil, top with fish, season with salt and pepper, and top with 2 lemon slices and 2 parsley sprigs. Fold the foil over securing completely, making a double fold in center and at both ends. Place on a baking sheet. Bake in a preheated 450° oven for 8 to 10 minutes or until puffed and fish is just cooked through. Serve a packet on each dinner plate, opening the packet at the table. Makes 2 servings.

Capered Sole
in Brown Lemon Butter

Lemon and capers give a fast uplift to fish fillets.

1 lemon
2 sole or turbot fillets (about 12
   ounces)
1 tablespoon flour

Salt and pepper, to taste
2 tablespoons butter or margarine
1½ tablespoons lemon juice
1 tablespoon extra large capers

Cut half the lemon into thin rounds for garnish. Peel remaining lemon and chop the fruit into ¼-inch pieces. Coat the fish very lightly with flour and season with salt and pepper to taste. Heat a large skillet over moderately high heat and add 1 tablespoon butter. Place fish in the pan and cook, turning to lightly brown both sides. Remove to a platter and keep warm. Add the remaining butter to the pan drippings and heat until butter turns golden brown. Add lemon juice, lemon bits, and capers and stir to blend. Spoon over fish and garnish with lemon slices. Makes 2 servings.

Mahi Mahi East West

Ginger, lemon grass, and garlic imbue fish fillets with a lively flavor.

2 teaspoons light soy sauce
1 teaspoon brown sugar
1 teaspoon chopped or grated
  ginger root
1 teaspoon chopped lemon grass

1 clove garlic, minced
2 (6-ounce) mahi mahi or salmon
  fillets
Chive blossoms or chopped chives,
  for garnish

Place the soy sauce, sugar, ginger, lemon grass, and garlic in a bowl and stir to mix. Add fish steaks; turn to coat. Cover and chill 2 hours or longer. Barbecue or broil, turning once, allowing 4 minutes per side, or until desired doneness. Garnish with chive blossoms or chopped chives. Makes 2 servings.

Pickled Salmon and Shrimp

A jar of pickled fish and shrimp makes a great treat for a summer supper. Accompany with a cucumber salad and sliced tomatoes and a crusty rye or egg bread.

2 pound salmon fillet
12 peppercorns
12 whole allspice
¾ teaspoon salt
1 small onion, sliced
1 lemon, sliced
Water

½ pound large raw shrimp,
*   unshelled (optional)*
1 small sweet red or white onion,
*   sliced*
1½ cups white wine vinegar
⅓ cup sugar
½ cup water
1 bay leaf

Place the salmon in a saucepan, add 6 each of the peppercorns and allspice, the salt, onion slices, lemon slices, and enough water to cover fish by 1 inch. Bring to a boil, add shrimp, and simmer very gently 5 minutes, or until fish is just set. Drain off the liquid and let fish cool. Remove the skin from the fish and break it into 1 by 2-inch chunks (approximately) along its natural seams. Alternate fish chunks, shrimp, and the sliced sweet onion in a half-gallon jar.

Combine wine vinegar, sugar, the ½ cup water, bay leaf, and the remaining peppercorns and allspice and bring to a boil; simmer until sugar is dissolved. Pour over the fish. Cover and chill at least 8 hours or up to 3 days. Makes 8 servings.

Grilled Gingered Salmon

This spunky ginger marinade is a natural with barbecued salmon steaks or fillets.

3 tablespoons light soy sauce
3 tablespoons rice or white wine
  vinegar
2 tablespoons grated fresh ginger
  root

2 cloves garlic, minced
1 tablespoon sesame oil
1 tablespoon canola oil
4 salmon steaks or fillets, about
  6 ounces each

Mix together the soy sauce, vinegar, ginger, garlic, and oils. Place the fish steaks in a shallow dish and pour the marinade over them. Turn to coat and let chill 1 hour for flavors to penetrate. Grill over hot coals or broil, turning to brown both sides and allowing about 4 to 5 minutes on a side or until desired doneness. Makes 4 servings.

Baked Salmon with Pistachio Aioli

This is an excellent, simple way to handle a chunk of fish which can be served either hot or cold. The garlicky nut mayonnaise is also a zestful accompaniment to cold cooked vegetables such as green beans, broccoli, or asparagus.

2 pound piece (or larger) salmon

Pistachio Aioli:
1 egg
1½ tablespoons fresh lemon juice
1½ tablespoons white wine vinegar

½ teaspoon salt
3 garlic cloves, minced
⅔ cup canola oil
⅓ cup olive oil
*⅓ cup pistachios or toasted pine
    nuts*

Place fish in an oiled baking pan and bake in a preheated 450° oven for 10 minutes per inch of thickness, or about 12 minutes if fish is 1¼ inches thick. Let cool a few minutes, then peel off skin.

Meanwhile, place in a blender container the egg, lemon juice, vinegar, salt, and garlic and blend a few seconds. With motor running, gradually pour in the oils in a fine, steady stream. When mixture is the consistency of mayonnaise, stir in the nuts and blend 1 second. Turn into a container, cover, and chill until serving time. Makes about 1¼ cups.

Divide salmon into serving size pieces and spoon a dollop of sauce on top. Makes 6 servings.

Gingered Snapper Pacific

Garnish this fast fish entrée with a choice of fresh fruit for a refreshing accent.

2 tablespoons dry sherry
1½ tablespoons soy sauce
1 tablespoon lime or lemon juice
1 clove garlic, minced
½ teaspoon chopped fresh ginger
   root

12 ounces snapper or turbot fillets
Sliced carambola (star fruit),
   papaya, orange, or kiwi fruit,
   for garnish

In a shallow baking dish, stir together the sherry, soy sauce, lime juice, garlic, and ginger root. Turn fish in the marinade, cover, and chill 30 minutes. Uncover and bake with marinade in a preheated 450° oven 8 to 10 minutes, allowing 10 minutes per inch thickness of fillets, spooning marinade over fillets halfway through cooking. Garnish each serving with a few slices of fruit. Makes 2 servings.

Sugar Snap and Scallop Stir-Fry

Accompany this delectable seafood stir-fry with hot steamed rice.

2 tablespoons canola or peanut oil
2 green onions, cut in ½-inch
  pieces
2 teaspoons grated ginger root
1 clove garlic, minced
¾ pound scallops or medium-size
  raw shrimp, peeled, slit
  lengthwise, and deveined
½ pound sugar snap peas or pea
  pods, trimmed
½ cup diced jicama or sliced water
  chestnuts
⅓ cup clam juice
1 teaspoon cornstarch
1 teaspoon cold water
1 teaspoon soy sauce
Dash hot pepper seasoning, if
  desired
4 to 5 sprigs cilantro

Heat oil in a wok or large skillet. Add the onions, ginger root, and garlic, and stir-fry 1 minute. Add scallops or shrimp and sauté until seafood changes color. Add sugar snaps, jicama, and clam juice, and let cook 1 minute, stirring constantly. Blend together the cornstarch, cold water, soy sauce, and pepper seasoning and stir into the seafood. Cook, stirring until thickened. Garnish with cilantro sprigs. Makes 2 servings.

Fisherman's Shellfish Platter

Wine-steeped shellfish makes a splendid winter feast. Whole steamed artichokes are an apropos starter and caramelized pears or baked apples make an excellent finish to the meal.

1 dozen mussels or small rock clams
6 large prawns
1 lobster tail, split
½ cup dry white vermouth or dry
*   white wine*

4 tablespoons chopped fresh
*   cilantro or parsley*
2 cloves garlic, minced
2 tablespoons unsalted butter
Lemon wedges

Scrub the shellfish thoroughly and place in a large soup kettle, along with the vermouth, 2 tablespoons of the cilantro, and the garlic. Cover and simmer for 5 to 10 minutes or until the mussel or clam shells open. Transfer to a large platter and spoon the juices on top. Heat the butter and the remaining cilantro until butter melts; spoon over the shellfish. Garnish with lemon wedges. Offer your guests dampened towels. Makes 2 servings.

Five Spice Game Hen with Fruit

Exotic spices glaze a little hen for an intriguing entrée to mate with tropical fruit.

2 Rock Cornish game hens, about
   1 pound, 6 ounces each
Pepper, to taste
1 teaspoon Chinese five spice
2 tablespoons soy sauce
2 tablespoons sherry
1 teaspoon chopped peeled ginger
   root

1 clove garlic, minced
1 teaspoon sesame oil
Fruit accompaniment: sliced
   papaya, kiwi fruit, carambola,
   or orange
1 lime, cut in wedges

Remove giblets from the game hens; rinse hens and pat dry. Rub the hens with pepper and five spice and place on a rack in a roasting pan. Roast in a preheated 375° oven for 15 minutes. Mix together the soy sauce, sherry, ginger, garlic, and oil and brush this basting sauce over the birds. Continue roasting 45 minutes longer or until drumstick moves easily. To serve, cut each hen in half, garnish each half with a few slices of fruit and accompany with a lime wedge. Makes 4 servings.

Roast Game Hens with Garlic Pistachio Sauce

Here's an elegant yet easy entrée for a guest dinner. Crunchy pistachios and caramelized garlic nuggets enhance the wine juices on roasted game hens.

2 game hens, about 1 pound,
    6 ounces each
1 tablespoon fresh tarragon or
    1 teaspoon dried tarragon
1 shallot, chopped
Salt and pepper, to taste
½ cup dry vermouth or dry white
    wine

16 cloves garlic, peeled
1 teaspoon butter
¼ cup shelled pistachios
½ cup chicken broth
2 tablespoons raspberry vinegar
2 tablespoons minced Italian
    parsley

Remove giblets from hens, rinse hens in cold water and pat dry. Tuck tarragon and shallot inside each cavity. Season hens with salt and pepper and place them in a shallow roasting pan. Roast in a preheated 375° oven for 30 minutes. Pour half the vermouth over the hens and continue roasting 30 minutes longer, basting with remaining vermouth, and cooking until drumsticks move easily.

Meanwhile, place the garlic cloves in a small saucepan and cover with water. Bring to a boil and simmer 5 minutes; drain and repeat process two more times. (Garlic should be soft.) Drain water. In a small saucepan, melt the butter. Add garlic and shake pan, sautéeing until garlic just turns pale golden brown. Add the pistachios and heat through. Remove garlic and nuts from pan and set aside.

Drain juices from game hens and skim fat. Pour juices into a saucepan, add chicken broth, and cook down until reduced by half. Add the vinegar and bring to a boil; then add garlic and nuts. Halve game hens and spoon sauce over them. Sprinkle with parsley. Makes 4 servings.

Note: If desired, arrange hens on a bed of radicchio or arugula to make a pretty plate.

Roast Chicken with Garlic

A golden bird makes a festive entrée for family dining. If desired, roast two broiler–fryers serving one and using the other for chicken salad, pitas, or fajitas.

3-pound broiler–fryer
Salt and pepper, to taste
1 tablespoon fresh tarragon or
    rosemary or ¾ teaspoon dried
    tarragon or rosemary

½ cup dry white vermouth
l large head or bulb garlic
1 teaspoon butter

Season chicken with salt and pepper and sprinkle tarragon inside the cavity. Place breast-side up on a rack in a roasting pan. Roast in a pre-heated 425° oven for 20 minutes. Turn chicken over, reduce heat to 375° and cook 1 hour longer, basting with vermouth, until the drumstick moves easily.

Meanwhile, separate the garlic head into cloves but do not peel the cloves. Simmer them in boiling water to cover for 5 minutes; drain completely and repeat this process twice; drain thoroughly. Let cool, then slip skins off the cloves. Sauté the cloves in butter for 2 to 3 minutes or until barely browned. Pour off pan juices from the roasted chicken and skim the fat. Carve the meat and scatter several garlic cloves over each serving. Pass pan juices. Makes 4 to 6 servings.

Roast Chicken with Grapes

Grapes burst with juiciness after roasting inside a bird. This is an easy-to-prepare dish with lots of flair.

3 pound broiler–fryer
1 tablespoon lemon juice
Salt, pepper, and paprika

1½ cups seedless grapes
2 teaspoons grated lemon zest
⅓ cup dry white wine

Wash the chicken and pat it dry. Place chicken on a rack in a roasting pan and rub the skin with lemon juice and sprinkle with salt, pepper, and paprika. Toss the grapes with lemon zest and tuck them inside the cavity. Roast in a preheated 425° oven for 15 minutes; reduce temperature to 375° and continue roasting 45 minutes to 1 hour longer, or until drumstick moves easily, basting several times with wine and drippings. Carve, and serve grapes alongside. Pass pan juices, skimmed of fat. Makes 4 servings.

Chicken Tandoori

Either chicken or turkey breast works well in this spicy Moroccan-style entrée. Accompany with couscous for a pleasing combination.

8 threads saffron
1 tablespoon coriander seeds
¾ teaspoon cumin seeds
2 whole cloves
Seeds of 2 cardamom pods
Small piece dried hot red pepper
¾ cup plain yogurt
½ medium onion, quartered

2 teaspoons chopped fresh ginger
   root
2 cloves garlic, peeled
4 split chicken breats, skinned or
   1½ pounds turkey breasts, cut
   in 4 cutlets, about ¾-inch thick
Lemon wedges, for garnish

Soak the saffron in 2 tablespoons hot water for a few minutes. Meanwhile, in a heavy skillet, toast the coriander and cumin seeds, cloves, cardamom, and pepper for 10 to 15 minutes over low heat, stirring or shaking the pan frequently.

Place the yogurt, onion, ginger, and garlic in a blender or food processor and blend until smooth. Add the toasted seeds and soaked saffron and liquid and blend smooth. Place the chicken pieces in a bowl and pour the marinade over them. Cover and refrigerate for at least 2 hours or overnight. Broil or barbecue over medium coals, turning to brown both sides, allowing about 15 to 20 minutes. Garnish with lemon wedges. Makes 4 servings.

Chicken Breasts with Chèvre and Sun-Dried Tomatoes

This fast, festive entrée is special enough to double or triple for impromptu guests.

2 split chicken breasts, boned
  (about 12 ounces)
2 tablespoons Dijon or
  stone-ground mustard
2 tablespoons lemon juice

1½ tablespoons chopped fresh
  mixed herbs (preferably two or
  three kinds): tarragon, thyme,
  chives, and Italian parsley
4 sun-dried tomatoes
2 ounces chèvre
6 to 8 sprigs arugula

Place the chicken breasts in a shallow dish. Mix together the mustard, lemon juice, and herbs and spread over each chicken breast. Cover and refrigerate 2 hours or overnight. Bake in a preheated 375° oven for 20 to 25 minutes or until cooked through. Add the tomatoes the last few minutes, just to heat them through. Arrange chicken on plates, top with the cheese, and tuck in arugula sprigs. Makes 2 servings.

Pistachio-Studded Chicken Terrine

This is an excellent terrine to accompany a soup or enjoy sliced in luncheon sandwiches.

1 large onion, finely chopped
2 teaspoons olive oil
1½ pounds chicken breasts, boned
    and skinned, or turkey breast
1 pound lean ground pork
1½ teaspoons salt
½ teaspoon dried thyme
½ teaspoon ground allspice
1 teaspoon freshly grated lemon
    zest
¼ teaspoon freshly ground pepper

¼ teaspoon ground nutmeg
1 egg
1 egg white
⅓ cup nonfat dry milk powder
⅓ cup chicken broth
2 tablespoons dry sherry
2 cloves garlic, minced
6 tablespoons pistachios
2 bay leaves
6 peppercorns

In a small skillet, sauté the onion in oil until soft. Grind the chicken or turkey in a food processor or food grinder. Place the sautéed onion, chicken, pork, salt, thyme, allspice, lemon zest, pepper, nutmeg, egg, egg white, milk powder, broth, sherry, and garlic in a bowl. Mix until blended. Spread half of the mixture in a greased 8 by 4½-inch loaf pan. Sprinkle with half the pistachios. Cover with remaining meat mixture and sprinkle with remaining nuts. Decorate the top with bay leaves and peppercorns. Cover with foil. Place in a pan containing 1 inch of water and bake in a preheated 325° oven for 1½ hours or until set. Remove from water and chill 1 day before serving. Makes 8 servings.

Hint: If desired, make 2 days in advance and chill.

Lemon and Herb-Basted Turkey Breast

A tangy lemon and fresh herb marinade permeates roast turkey for a treat to serve hot or cold.

1 turkey breast, about 4 to 6 pounds

Marinade:
2 lemons
2 tablespoons fresh rosemary or
* 1 teaspoon dried rosemary*

2 tablespoons fresh oregano or
* 1 teaspoon dried oregano*
2 tablespoons Dijon mustard
½ cup white wine
Salt and pepper, to taste
2 cloves garlic, minced

Place the turkey skin side down in a baking dish. Peel the lemons with a vegetable peeler, julienne the peel in fine strips, and then juice the lemons. Place the lemon juice, lemon zest, herbs, mustard, wine, salt and pepper, and garlic in a bowl. Mix together and spoon half of the mixture over the turkey breast, cover, and chill overnight.

To cook, place turkey on a rack in a roasting pan and place in a pre-heated 375° oven. Bake turkey breast about 1½ to 2 hours or until meat thermometer registers 160°. During baking, baste with remaining marinade and if necessary add water to pan to keep from drying out. Serve on a board garnished with rosemary sprigs and lemons. Makes 8 to 10 servings.

Wine-Glazed Turkey Drumsticks

Herb-seasoned turkey drumsticks are excellent hot or cold. It is just as easy to do a double recipe at a time.

2 turkey drumsticks, about
   12 ounces each
Zest of 1 lemon, julienned
1½ tablespoons lemon juice
½ cup dry red wine
½ cup dry red wine
1 tablespoon olive oil

1 tablespoon fresh rosemary or
   ¾ teaspoon dried rosemary
2 tablespoons chopped parsley
1 shallot or green onion, chopped
1 clove garlic, minced
Salt and pepper, to taste
1 lemon, thinly sliced and seeded

Skin the turkey pieces. In a bowl, mix together the lemon zest, lemon juice, wine, oil, rosemary, parsley, shallot, garlic, and salt and pepper. Place the turkey pieces in a plastic bag and pour the marinade over them. Seal the bag and refrigerate for 4 hours or longer.

To cook, place turkey in a baking dish and add lemon slices. Pour half the marinade over the turkey and bake in a preheated 375° oven for 1½ hours or until cooked through and meat thermometer registers 170°. Baste with remaining marinade during baking and, if necessary, add water to pan to keep from drying out. Makes 2 servings.

Turkey Spiedini

Typically made with veal, turkey works admirably in these neat, fast pinwheels for a stylish entrée with appeal. The word *spiedini* is Italian for food cooked on a skewer.

12 ounces thinly sliced turkey breast cutlets, about ¼ inch thick (or use veal cutlets)
2 tablespoons Dijon or Parisian mustard
2 ounces prosciutto, very thinly sliced
2 ounces fontina, Gruyère, or Jarlsberg cheese or low-fat Swiss cheese

2 tablespoons chopped Italian parsley
1 teaspoon fresh oregano
2 teaspoons melted butter or olive oil
1½ tablespoons lemon juice
1 clove garlic, minced
Freshly ground pepper, to taste

Cut turkey meat into approximately 2½ by 5-inch rectangles to make about 8 pieces, allowing about 4 turkey pinwheels per serving. Lay the turkey pieces flat on a board and spread lightly with mustard. Cut prosciutto and cheese into as many pieces as turkey strips and lay a prosciutto slice and cheese slice on top of each turkey strip. Sprinkle with parsley and oregano. Roll up and skewer turkey bundles placing 4 on each skewer.

Mix together the butter, lemon juice, garlic, and pepper, and brush over each pinwheel. Place skewers on a rack on a broiling pan. Broil about 4 to 6 inches from the heat until golden, then turn and broil the other side, allowing about 4 to 5 minutes on each side to cook through. Makes 2 servings.

Turkey and Mushrooms Dijon

Using French seasonings instead of Oriental ones, here is a quick stir-fry with turkey breast and mushrooms. Another time substitute veal for the turkey.

1 shallot, finely chopped
1 clove garlic, minced
¼ pound mushrooms, thinly sliced
3 teaspoons olive oil
12 ounces turkey breast slices,
    about ⅛ inch thick
1 tablespoon cornstarch

Salt and pepper, to taste
⅔ cup dry white wine
2 teaspoons Dijon mustard
½ teaspoon anchovy paste
1 tablespoon minced parsley
1 tablespoon minced chives or
    green onion tops

Using a large non-stick skillet or wok, quickly sauté the shallot, garlic, and mushrooms in 1½ teaspoons of oil, stirring, just until heated through; turn the mushrooms out onto a platter. Dip the turkey in a mixture of cornstarch, salt, and pepper, and stir-fry in the remaining 1½ teaspoons of oil, just until browned on both sides. Pour the wine into the pan drippings and cook down until turkey is cooked through and juices are reduced by half. Stir in the mustard and anchovy paste. Return mushrooms to the pan and heat through. Divide stir-fry between 2 plates and sprinkle with parsley and chives. Makes 2 servings.

Turkey Piccata

Capers and lemon uplift turkey slices for a piquant variation on the traditional veal scallopini.

12 ounces turkey breast slices
2 tablespoons cornstarch
Salt and pepper, to taste
1 tablespoon olive oil
1 tablespoon butter
Juice of 1 lemon
¼ pound button mushrooms,
    thinly sliced

1 clove garlic, minced
2 tablespoons capers
1 teaspoon fresh oregano or
    ¼ teaspoon dried oregano
½ cup dry white wine
1 lemon, thinly sliced and seeded

Make 2 or 3 cuts on membrane of outer edges of turkey slices to prevent them from curling. Dredge each slice with cornstarch seasoned with salt and pepper and pound between 2 sheets of waxed paper to a very thin, even thickness, about ⅛ inch thick. Cut larger pieces in 2 pieces if desired.

In a large skillet, heat half the oil and butter over medium heat and quickly sauté the turkey slices until lightly browned, turning once. Add half the lemon juice and cook until turkey is just done. Remove turkey from skillet to a warm platter. Add the remaining oil and butter and sauté the mushrooms and garlic until glazed. Add capers, oregano, and wine and remaining lemon juice. Bring to a boil, scrape up browned bits from pan, and reduce juices slightly. Return turkey to pan, scatter the lemon slices over the turkey, and heat through. Makes 2 servings.

Gingered Turkey Patties

These meat patties are chock full of flavor and are excellent hot or cold.

1 pound ground turkey
1 shallot, chopped
2 cloves garlic, chopped
2 tablespoons chopped parsley
2 teaspoons chopped fresh ginger
   root
½ teaspoon ground allspice

Salt and pepper, to taste
⅓ cup dry red wine or dry sherry
2 tablespoons Dijon mustard
12 soft sun-dried tomatoes
   (optional)
4 ounces low-fat Monterey Jack or
   Muenster cheese (optional)

In a bowl, mix together the turkey, shallot, garlic, parsley, ginger, allspice, salt and pepper, and wine. Shape into small 2½-inch patties. Place on a broiling rack and broil about 4 to 5 minutes on each side or until cooked through. Spread with mustard and serve hot or cold. If desired, top each patty with a sun-dried tomato half and a slice of low-fat Monterey Jack or Muenster cheese the last minute of cooking. Makes 3 servings.

Smoked Almond Turkey Terrine

This savory meat loaf is excellent for dinner or serve it sliced in sandwiches.

1 large onion, finely chopped
2 cloves garlic, minced
¼ cup dry sherry
1 pound ground turkey
1 pound ground pork
1 teaspoon salt
½ teaspoon dried thyme
½ teaspoon ground allspice

½ teaspoon freshly grated lemon zest
¼ teaspoon freshly ground pepper
2 egg whites
¼ cup non-fat dry milk powder
2 tablespoons minced parsley
⅓ cup smoked almonds

In a small saucepan, place the onion, garlic, and sherry and simmer until onion is soft and wine is reduced to a glaze; let cool. In a bowl, place the ground meats, salt, thyme, allspice, lemon zest, pepper, egg whites, dry milk, parsley, and onion mixture and mix until blended. Pat half the mixture into an oiled 9 by 5-inch loaf pan. Dot with half the almonds. Cover with remaining meat; pat smooth and dot with almonds. Bake the meat loaf in a preheated 350° oven for 1 hour or until set. Let cool and chill. Slice thinly and serve with mustard. Makes 8 servings.

Grilled Burgers with Herbs

Use fresh herbs from the garden or market to enliven everyday grilled turkey burgers.

¾ pound ground turkey
1 egg white
1 shallot or green onion, chopped
1 clove garlic, minced

2 tablespoons chopped Italian
  parsley
Salt and pepper, to taste
Herb Dressing (recipe follows)

In a bowl, mix the meat with egg white, shallot, garlic, parsley, and salt and pepper. Shape into two patties. Broil until browned; turn over and brown the other side and cook until done, allowing about 4 minutes per side. Transfer to plates and spoon the Herb Dressing over the patties. Makes 2 servings.

HERB DRESSING:

2 tablespoons chopped Italian
  parsley
1 shallot, chopped

1 teaspoon fresh oregano or thyme
  or ¼ teaspoon dried oregano
  or thyme
1½ tablespoons lemon juice

Mix the dressing ingredients in a small bowl.

Fillets with Gorgonzola

Creamy Gorgonzola or another fine blue cheese like Danish Blue Castello gives an elegant touch to grilled steak.

2 beef fillets, about 6 ounces each
1 tablespoon lemon juice
2 tablespoons balsamic vinegar
2 tablespoons olive oil
1 clove garlic, minced

Salt and pepper, to taste
3 ounces Gorgonzola or Danish
  Blue Castello
Watercress, for garnish

Place the meat in a plastic bag. Mix together the lemon juice, vinegar, oil, and garlic and pour over the meat. Seal the bag and let the meat marinate 2 hours or longer. Grill meat over medium-hot coals or broil, turning to brown both sides and cooking until medium rare or desired doneness. Season with salt and pepper. Transfer meat to plates and top with pieces of cheese. Garnish with watercress sprigs. Makes 2 servings.

Stir-Fry Steak and Mushrooms

This fast stir-fry lends itself to many vegetable variations. Toss in some diced jicama for crunch or vary the kind of mushroom with the availability.

1 teaspoon olive oil
1 teaspoon sesame oil
2 shallots, chopped
1 teaspoon ginger root
1 clove garlic, minced

¾ pound lean beef sirloin strips,
   cut for stir-fry
¾ pound button mushrooms or
   oyster mushrooms, sliced
¾ cup diced jicama (optional)
1 tablespoon balsamic vinegar

In a large skillet, heat olive oil and sesame oil over moderate heat and sauté shallots, ginger root, and garlic until soft. Add beef and stir-fry 2 minutes, just until it loses its pink color. Push to sides of pan. Add mushrooms and jicama and sauté 1 minute. Add vinegar and heat through, stirring. Makes 2 servings.

Steak and Vegetable Stir-Fry

A variety of seasonal vegetables can enhance this fast stir-fry.

¾ pound flank or skirt steak
2 tablespoons oil
2 cloves garlic, minced
1 teaspoon chopped fresh ginger
  root
1½ cups thin sliced vegetables:
  asparagus, snow peas,
  mushrooms, celery, red
  peppers, or carrots

¼ cup dry sherry or broth
2 tablespoons oyster sauce
Dash of red pepper flakes
½ teaspoon brown sugar
¼ cup pistachios

Cut the steak across the grain into ⅜ inch thick slices. In a wok or large skillet, heat 1 tablespoon of the oil, add garlic and ginger and sauté briefly. Add steak slices and quickly brown all sides, stirring constantly. Remove meat and reserve. Heat remaining oil and sauté vegetables until crisp-tender, about 2 minutes. Remove vegetables and reserve with meat. Add sherry, oyster sauce, pepper flakes, and sugar to the pan; stir and cook about 2 minutes. Add steak, vegetables, and nuts and mix to heat through. Makes 2 servings.

Appetizer: Crudités with Tomato and Basil Cheese Spread and Shiitake Mushroom Spread.

Soup: Golden Squash and Pesto.

Salad: Lemon Grass Tabbouleh with Shrimp and Grapes (or Cherry Tomatoes).

Pizza: Tortilla Flats.

*Entrée: Fisherman's
Shellfish Platter.*

House Staple: Couscous–Stuffed Grape Leaves.

Bread: Garlic and Rosemary Whole-wheat Rounds.

Dessert: Caramel Cookie Baskets with Berries and Sherbet.

Fajitas

Either beef steak or turkey works well in this Southwestern sandwich. Salsa or guacamole is a great accompaniment.

12 ounces skirt steaks or boneless turkey breast, sliced ½ inch thick
1 tablespoon olive oil
2 cloves garlic, minced
1 shallot, chopped
¼ cup dry red or white wine
Cilantro Sesame Sauce (recipe follows)
4 (6-inch) flour tortillas

Place the skirt steaks or turkey in a baking dish and coat with a mixture of oil, garlic, shallot, and red wine for beef or white wine for turkey. Chill 1 hour. Grill over medium hot coals until browned and cooked to desired doneness, turning once.

Meanwhile, prepare Cilantro Sesame Sauce. Wrap tortillas in foil and warm on the grill. Slice meat thinly on the diagonal, distribute on the hot tortillas, and top with Cilantro Sesame Sauce. Makes 2 servings.

CILANTRO SESAME SAUCE:

⅔ cup chopped cilantro
2 teaspoons sesame oil
¾ cup chopped red onions

Mix sauce ingredients together in a small bowl.

Far Eastern London Broil

Oriental flavors permeate grilled steak for a versatile entrée that is excellent hot or cold.

2 tablespoons soy sauce
¼ cup dry sherry
1 tablespoon sesame oil
2 cloves garlic, minced

1 teaspoon grated fresh ginger root
1 London broil (top round steak) or
*   flank steak, about 1½ pounds*

Mix together the soy sauce, wine, oil, garlic, and ginger root in a bowl. Place the meat in a zip-lock plastic bag, pour the marinade over the meat, seal the bag, and refrigerate for 1 to 2 hours. Broil or barbecue the meat over low coals, cooking until medium rare, about 8 minutes on each side. Makes 4 to 6 servings.

Joe's Special

An old-time specialty from New Joe's North Beach Italian Restaurant in San Francisco, this scramble of ground beef or turkey, spinach, and egg is a fine spur-of-the-moment entrée.

2 green onions, chopped
¼ pound mushrooms, sliced
1 teaspoon olive oil
¾ pound lean ground beef or
   turkey
2 cloves garlic, minced

Salt and pepper, to taste
1 small bunch spinach, finely
   chopped
2 eggs
2 tablespoons shredded Romano or
   Parmesan cheese

In a large skillet, sauté the onions and mushrooms in oil until soft. Push to the sides of·the pan, add ground beef or turkey, garlic, and salt and pepper and cook until meat is browned. Mix in the spinach and cook for 2 minutes, just until spinach wilts. Break the eggs over the mixture and stir to mix in and cook through. Sprinkle with cheese. Makes 2 to 3 servings.

Greek Meat Sauce

This lively meat sauce has multiple uses. It's a favorite from Yaya — my mother-in-law. Make it with your preferred ground meat. Long, slow cooking mellows the flavors to a savory, caramel-like goodness.

3 medium onions, finely chopped
3 pounds lean ground beef, ground
    turkey, or 1½ pounds each
    ground turkey and pork
3 cloves garlic, minced
3 (6-ounce) cans tomato paste
1 stick cinnamon

1½ teaspoons whole mixed pickling
    spices, tied in a cheesecloth bag
1½ teaspoons salt
Freshly ground pepper
½ cup dry red wine
1 cup water

Place the onions, meat, garlic, tomato paste, cinnamon stick, bag of pickling spice, salt, pepper, wine, and water in a large Dutch oven or large saucepan. Stir to mix well. Cover and simmer gently, stirring occasionally, for 3 hours, or until sauce is thickened. Or bake in a preheated 275° oven for 3 hours. Let the sauce cool, skim the fat, and ladle into containers. Refrigerate or freeze. Makes about 4 pints.

Hint: The sauce may be frozen for up to 1 month.

Saucy Italian Green Beans

Caramelized meat sauce tops green beans for a fast flourish.

12 ounces Italian or regular green
  beans
1 pint Greek Meat Sauce
  (see page 132)
1 green onion, chopped

⅓ cup shredded Romano or
  Parmesan cheese
2 tablespoons roasted sunflower
  seeds
Yogurt or sliced avocado, for
  garnish (optional)

Trim ends from the beans and cut beans diagonally in 1½-inch lengths. Cook the beans in boiling salted water for 5 to 7 minutes or until barely tender; drain. Or microwave beans on high for 4 to 5 minutes until barely tender. Heat meat sauce in a saucepan until heated through or heat in a microwave for 3 minutes or until hot. Spoon the beans onto 2 dinner plates, top with meat sauce, and sprinkle with green onion, cheese, and sunflower seeds. If desired, add a dollop of yogurt or a few slices of avocado for garnish. Makes 2 servings.

Turkish-Slashed Eggplant

The small slender eggplants make handsome individual servings topped with meat sauce.

2 slender eggplants, about 6 to 7
    inches long
Salt
1 pint Greek Meat Sauce
    (see page 132)

½ cup tomato sauce
⅓ cup shredded Romano or
    Parmesan cheese
2 tablespoons chopped Italian
    parsley

Slit the eggplants lengthwise to within 1 inch of the ends. Sprinkle with salt and set aside for 20 minutes. Rinse eggplants, pat dry, and place in a baking dish. Cover and bake in a preheated 400° oven for 30 minutes or microwave on high for 5 to 7 minutes. Remove from oven and fill each slash with Greek Meat Sauce. Sprinkle with cheese. Pour tomato sauce around the eggplants. Continue baking 20 minutes longer or microwave 2 to 3 minutes longer, or until heated through. Sprinkle parsley over the top. Serve hot or warm. Makes 2 servings.

Veal Cordon Bleu

It's easy to stuff veal with prosciutto and cheese to give it a special flair.

12 ounces veal steak or cutlets, top
   sirloin, or turkey breast cutlets
Salt and pepper, to taste
1 to 2 ounces Gruyère or Jarlsberg
   cheese
2 slices prosciutto or boiled ham
1 teaspoon olive oil

½ cup beef or chicken stock
2 tablespoons red or white wine
   vinegar
1 tablespoon chopped Italian
   parsley
1 tablespoon chopped chives or
   green onion tops

Cut a pocket in one side of each steak, making an opening to within ½ inch of the other three sides. Season meat with salt and pepper. Slip a slice of cheese and a slice of ham inside each steak pocket. Heat a large skillet with oil and pan fry steak until browned; turn and brown other side, cooking meat to desired doneness. Remove to a platter and keep warm. Add the broth and vinegar to the skillet and cook down until slightly reduced. Add parsley and chives and spoon the sauce over the meat. Makes 2 servings.

Veal Loaf Cordon Bleu

A colorful stripe of cheese, prosciutto, and herbs ribbons this cold meat loaf.

1 bunch green onions, chopped
1 teaspoon olive oil
2 slices sourdough French bread,
    cubed or ¼ cup wheat germ
3 tablespoons dry sherry
⅓ cup chicken broth
2 eggs
1 teaspoon salt
¼ teaspoon freshly ground pepper
1 teaspoon dry mustard

2 teaspoons fresh oregano or
    ½ teaspoon dried oregano
2 cloves garlic, minced
6 tablespoons chopped parsley
1½ pounds ground veal
½ pound ground pork
1 cup shredded Jarlsberg or
    Gruyère cheese (about 4
    ounces) or low-fat cheese
3 ounces prosciutto, thinly sliced

In a small skillet, sauté the green onions in oil over medium heat until soft; set aside. In a mixing bowl, mix together the bread or wheat germ, sherry, broth, eggs, salt, pepper, mustard, oregano, garlic, and 3 tablespoons of the parsley. Add the ground meats and mix until blended. In a greased 9 by 13-inch baking pan, pat out half the meat mixture into a rectangle about 6 by 10 inches. Mix together the sautéed onions, cheese, prosciutto, and the remaining 3 tablespoons parsley and pat this over the meat. Pat out remaining meat on a sheet of waxed paper, making another 6 by 10-inch rectangle. Lay this over the cheese and ham filling and press the edges of the meat layers together, forming a compact, rounded loaf. Bake in a preheated 350° oven for 1 hour or until juices no longer run pink. Serve hot or chilled. Makes 8 servings.

Veal and Apricot Tajine

A melange of spices, honey, lime, and pistachios in the Moroccan style provides delicious overtones on nuggets of veal or turkey. If using turkey, choose the dark meat, such as a boneless thigh, for flavorful, moist morsels.

1 small onion, chopped
1 teaspoon shredded fresh ginger
   root
1 stick cinnamon
⅛ teaspoon turmeric
1 teaspoon olive oil
1 clove garlic, minced
1 pound veal or·uncooked dark
   turkey meat (boneless thigh),
   cut in 1¼-inch cubes

Salt and freshly ground pepper, to
   taste
12 dried apricot halves
1 tablespoon honey
1½ tablespoons lime or lemon juice
2 tablespoons chopped pistachios
   or toasted almonds
Sprigs of cilantro or Italian
   parsley, for garnish
Lime or lemon wedges

Using a heavy oven-proof saucepan or Dutch oven, sauté the onion, ginger, cinnamon, and turmeric in oil until glazed. Add the garlic, veal or turkey, salt, and pepper and sauté a few minutes. Cover and bake in a preheated 325° oven for 40 minutes or until meat is cooked through and no longer pink inside. Remove from oven and add apricot halves. On cooktop, bring the stew to a boil and reduce any juices slightly. Add honey and lime juice to pan drippings, stir to coat the meat, and heat. To serve, sprinkle with nuts and garnish with cilantro sprigs and lime wedges. Makes 4 servings.

Butterflied Lamb

Butterflying a leg of lamb makes it easy to cook evenly on the grill. Here it can make a double entrée, hot and barbecued and sliced cold in a fruited salad.

1 small leg of lamb, boned and
* butterflied (about 4 to*
* 4½ pounds)*
1 cup dry red wine
3 tablespoons olive oil
4 cloves garlic, minced

2 tablespoons fresh rosemary or
* 2 teaspoons dried rosemary*
2 tablespoons chopped parsley
Salt and pepper, to taste
3 lemons, cut in half on a zigzag
Rosemary sprigs, for garnish

Have your butcher bone and butterfly the leg of lamb. Place the meat in a zip-lock bag. Mix together the wine, oil, garlic, rosemary, parsley, and salt and pepper, and pour on the meat. Seal the bag securely. Marinate, chilled, for several hours or overnight. Barbecue the lamb over medium coals, turning once, until medium-rare, about 8 to 10 minutes on a side, depending on thickness. Slice thinly. Place on a board and garnish with lemon halves and rosemary sprigs. Makes 6 to 8 servings.

Lamb Chops with Ratatouille Relish

A ratatouille-style crispy relish partners with lamb for a pleasing accompaniment.

2 round bone lamb chops
2 tablespoons lemon juice
1 tablespoon olive oil
2 cloves garlic, minced
2 teaspoons fresh oregano or
   ½ teaspoon dried oregano
1 shallot, chopped

2 tablespoons olive oil
1 small zucchini, diced
1 small Japanese eggplant, diced
1 small red pepper, diced
2 tablespoons chopped Italian
   parsley
Salt and pepper, to taste

Let lamb chops marinate in a mixture of the lemon juice, oil, garlic, and oregano for 1 hour. Broil or grill meat over medium hot coals, turning to brown both sides and cooking until medium rare, about 10 to 12 minutes. Meanwhile, in a large skillet over medium high heat, sauté the shallot in oil until glazed. Add the zucchini and eggplant and sauté until crisp tender. Add pepper and parsley and heat through, about 1 minute. Season with salt and pepper. Serve chops with relish alongside. Makes 2 servings.

Grilled Lamb
and Vegetable Kebabs

With this recipe it is smart to skewer the vegetables separately from the herb-scented lamb to control the cooking time of each.

⅓ cup dry white wine
2 tablespoons olive oil
2 tablespoons lemon juice
2 cloves garlic, minced
2 teaspoons crumbled fresh
    rosemary or ½ teaspoon dried
    rosemary
Salt and pepper, to taste

1½ pounds boneless lamb, cut in
    about 1½-inch cubes or
    4 lamb steaks
1 small slender eggplant, cut in
    ½-inch slices
1 red pepper halved, seeded, and
    cut in 1-inch strips
1 gold or green pepper, seeded,
    and cut in 1-inch strips
2 small onions, quartered

For the marinade, combine the wine, oil, lemon juice, garlic, rosemary, and salt and pepper in a bowl. Place lamb in another bowl and pour half the marinade over it. Let stand 1 hour. Add the vegetables to the remaining marinade and turn to coat. When ready to grill, skewer meat on 4 skewers and alternate vegetables on separate skewers. Grill over medium hot coals for 10 to 15 minutes, or until meat is medium rare and vegetables are crisp tender. Makes 4 servings.

Lamb Bandit Style

In the Greek tradition, the meat and vegetables are sealed and cooked "bandit style." For a charming first course, start with stuffed grapes leaves and Greek olives.

2 round bone lamb chops
Salt and pepper to taste
2 teaspoons fresh oregano or
½ teaspoon crumbled dried
oregano
1 clove garlic, minced
2 small zucchini, halved lengthwise

2 small yellow squash, halved
lengthwise
2 green onions, chopped
1 ounce feta cheese, crumbled
1½ tablespoons lemon juice
1 tablespoon olive oil

Season the chops with salt, pepper, oregano, and garlic. Place each on a 12-inch sheet of parchment paper or foil. Lay zucchini and yellow squash on top. Scatter onions and crumbled cheese over the top. Drizzle with lemon juice and oil. Double fold parchment or foil and secure with paper clips. Place packets on a baking pan and bake in a preheated 350° oven for 1 hour. To serve, place sealed packets on dinner plates. Makes 2 servings.

Sprouted Lamb Loaves

Interchange the meats to suit your whim or dietary desires. The little meat loaves are excellent hot or cold.

*1½ pounds lean ground lamb,
    veal, or turkey
½ pound ground pork
2 shallots, chopped
3 tablespoons chopped parsley
1 cup chopped alfalfa sprouts
⅓ cup toasted wheat germ
⅓ cup dry sherry or chicken broth*

*2 eggs
2 teaspoons freshly grated orange
    zest
2 cloves garlic, minced
1 tablespoon fresh oregano,
    chopped or 1 teaspoon dried
    oregano
Salt and pepper, to taste*

In a bowl, mix together the ground lamb, pork, shallots, parsley, sprouts, wheat germ, sherry, eggs, orange peel, garlic, oregano, and salt and pepper to taste. Spoon into small greased muffin tins. Bake in a preheated 375° oven for 20 to 25 minutes, or until lightly browned and completely cooked through. Serve hot or cold. Makes 6 to 8 servings.

Hint: May be prepared 1 or 2 days in advance.

Gingered Pork with Pistachios

Golden raisins and pistachios stud this rolled pork loin for a flavorful entrée.

4 pound pork loin, boned
3 cloves garlic, minced
2 teaspoons green peppercorns
⅓ cup pistachios
⅓ cup golden raisins
4 tablespoons Dijon mustard
2 tablespoons soy sauce

2 teaspoons chopped fresh ginger
  root
2 teaspoons grated lemon zest
Watercress or parsley sprigs, for
  garnish
Lime or lemon wedges

Lay the meat out flat on a board and sprinkle it with half the garlic, the peppercorns, pistachios, and raisins. Roll the meat up and tie it with a string. Mix together the mustard, soy sauce, ginger root, lemon zest, and remaining garlic and spread the mixture over the surface of the roast. Place in a roasting pan, insert a meat thermometer, and roast in a preheated 325° oven until temperature registers 160°, about 1½ hours. Remove meat to a platter and serve hot, sliced and garnished with watercress and citrus wedges. Or serve cold. Makes about 8 servings.

Moo Shu Pork

Here's a fun, simplified Oriental dish to tuck into flour tortillas.

6 small flour tortillas
2 green onions
3 teaspoons canola oil
1 teaspoon sesame oil
½ pound pork tenderloin, cut in
  ⅛ inch thick strips or 2 pork
  chops, boned and trimmed
1 teaspoon grated ginger root
1 clove garlic, minced

¼ pound button mushrooms, sliced
½ cup sliced bamboo shoots or
  water chestnuts
1 inner stalk celery, thinly sliced
  diagonally
2 teaspoons light soy sauce
½ teaspoon brown sugar
2 eggs, lightly beaten

Wrap the tortillas in foil and heat in a preheated 350° oven for 10 minutes.

Cut the onions in 1½-inch lengths and cut 1 end of each lengthwise, making several ¼-inch slashes. Place onions in a bowl of ice water and let stand 5 to 10 minutes to fan out.

Heat 2 teaspoons of the canola oil and the teaspoon of sesame oil in a large skillet. Add the pork and ginger and stir-fry 2 minutes. Add garlic, mushrooms, bamboo shoots, and celery and stir-fry 1 minute. Add soy sauce and sugar and heat, stirring until blended. Heat remaining 1 teaspoon oil in a small skillet. Pour in beaten eggs and scramble until barely set. Spoon eggs onto a platter, cover with pork mixture, and surround with onion fans. Serve with hot tortillas. Makes 2 servings.

Note: If desired, substitute 3 dry shiitake mushrooms for the button mushrooms. Place shiitakes in a small bowl, cover with water, and let stand 15 minutes. Drain and chop coarsely and heat with pork.

Pork Patties California

A zestful topping of mustard, Monterey Jack cheese, and dried tomatoes elevates a broiled ground meat patty.

¾ pound ground pork, veal, or
   turkey
1 egg white
2 tablespoons dry sherry
2 cloves garlic, minced
2 tablespoons chopped Italian
   parsley
1 teaspoon chopped fresh oregano
   or thyme

¼ teaspoon ground allspice
¼ teaspoon freshly ground pepper
2 tablespoons stone-ground
   mustard
2 ounces sliced Monterey Jack or
   Jarlsberg cheese
4 sun-dried tomatoes

Mix the meat with egg white, sherry, garlic, parsley, oregano, allspice, and pepper. Pat into four patties about ½ inch thick. Place on a broiler pan and broil 3 to 4 minutes on a side or until cooked through. Spread each patty with mustard, top with cheese and tomatoes, and return to the oven just until cheese melts. Makes 2 servings.

Hot Sausages and Grapes

Glazed hot grapes lend instant flair to specialty sausages.

*2 Bratwurst or specialty sausages
    such as chicken, apple, or pork
    with herbs (about 12 ounces)*
1 teaspoon butter or margarine

*¼ pound seedless green or red
    grapes*
2 tablespoons dry white wine

Place the sausages in a saucepan and cover with water. Bring to a boil and let simmer very gently for 10 minutes or until cooked through; drain. Add butter to skillet and sauté the sausages until browned on both sides. Add the grapes and cook until heated through. Add wine and cook until juices are reduced. Spoon sausages and grapes onto hot plates. Makes 2 servings.

Sausages and Spuds in a Bag

Dinner bakes in a brown lunch bag and goes to the table enclosed, letting the wonderful aromas explode as the bag is opened.

2 lunch-size brown paper bags
Olive oil
2 medium Yukon gold or russet
   baking potatoes
Salt and pepper, to taste
1 clove garlic, minced

1 shallot, chopped
1 teaspoon fresh rosemary
1 tablespoon olive oil
2 mild Italian sausages or specialty
   sausages such as chicken,
   apple, or smoked bratwurst

Lightly oil the inside bottom of paper bags and place on a baking pan. Peel and slice the potatoes and season with salt and pepper. Toss potatoes with garlic, shallot, rosemary, and olive oil. Distribute the potatoes between the two bags and place sausages on top. Fold down bag tops and secure each with 2 paper clips. Bake in a preheated 375° oven for 1 hour or until potatoes and sausages are cooked through. Serve on dinner plates. Makes 2 servings.

Roasted Italian Sausages with Peppers

Red and gold pepper strips adorn hot juicy sausages. If desired for an appetizer, slice the sausages, serve on a platter with the peppers, and provide toothpicks to spear the sausages and peppers.

¾ pound mild Italian sausages
1 each red and gold bell pepper

With a fork, prick the surface of the sausages in about four places. Place in a baking pan. Cut peppers into sixths, remove seeds, and arrange them in the pan alongside the sausages. Bake in a preheated 350° oven for 40 minutes or until sausages are cooked through, turning them once. Serve sausages with peppers alongside as an entrée or serve as an appetizer. Makes 2 to 3 entrée servings or about 8 appetizer servings.

Greek Sausages

Orange zest, cinnamon, and allspice scent these garlic-imbued meat patties that are excellent hot or cold.

1 pound ground pork
1 pound ground veal or turkey
¾ teaspoon ground cinnamon
¾ teaspoon ground allspice
½ teaspoon salt
½ teaspoon freshly ground black
* pepper*

3 cloves garlic, minced
3 tablespoons orange zest, finely
* chopped*
½ cup dry white wine
1 tablespoon olive oil

Mix together the ground meats, cinnamon, allspice, salt, pepper, garlic, orange zest, and wine. Pat into small flat 1¾- or 2-inch patties. Heat oil in a large frying pan and sauté patties, turning to brown both sides and cooking through. If desired, deglaze pan with additional wine. Makes about 18 patties or 6 servings.

Vegetables and Accompaniments

Fresh cooked seasonal vegetables from the market or farmers' market augment the dinner plate with color, flavor, and nutrition. The working cook can also take advantage of some grains that lend themselves to freezing to compensate for their slow cooking time. Brown and wild rice can be oven-baked and packed in small containers or freezer bags, frozen, and be ready for microwaving. Couscous is the speed demon in grain cookery as it simply needs to stand a few minutes in steamy water to plump up to perfection. And don't overlook the microwave for "baking" potatoes in a jiffy.

Asparagus with Browned Nut Butter

A simple browned nut butter gilds asparagus with a tantalizing taste.

1½ pounds asparagus
4 tablespoons unsalted butter

3 tablespoons sliced almonds
3 tablespoons chopped parsley

Trim the ends from the asparagus. With a vegetable peeler, trim off the tough outer skin on the lower part of the stalks. Cook in a large pot of boiling salted water until crisp tender, about 5 to 7 minutes; drain. Heat the butter in a small pan until it bubbles, add nuts, and let simmer until butter starts to brown slightly. Pour over the asparagus. Sprinkle with parsley. Makes 4 servings.

Asparagus with Kasseri

Kasseri cheese and browned butter give a fast and elegant flourish to asparagus.

¾ pound fresh asparagus
2 tablespoons unsalted butter

¼ cup finely grated Kasseri, dry Monterey Jack, or Romano cheese

Cut off the tough ends of the asparagus and use a vegetable peeler to peel the lower part of the stalks. Cook in boiling salted water until just barely tender, about 5 to 7 minutes; drain. Place the asparagus on a platter or plates and keep warm. In a small saucepan, heat the butter until it sizzles and starts to turn brown; pour it over the asparagus and sprinkle with cheese. Makes 2 servings.

Asparagus Open – Sesame

This Oriental dressing refreshes cold boiled asparagus. Try it with other cold vegetables as well.

¾ pound asparagus spears
1 tablespoon lemon juice
1 tablespoon sesame oil
1 tablespoon white wine vinegar
2 tablespoons chopped cilantro

1 shallot or green onion (white
*   part only), chopped*
Dash each: salt, cayenne, oregano,
*   and cumin*
Edible nasturtiums, if desired

Trim the ends from the asparagus and plunge into boiling salted water. Cook 5 to 7 minutes or until al dente; drain and chill. Combine lemon juice, oil, vinegar, cilantro, shallot, salt, cayenne, oregano, and cumin and spoon over the asparagus. Garnish the plate with an edible nasturtium, if desired. Makes 2 servings.

Green Beans with Tarragon

The elfin French green beans are excellent dressed with herbs.

1 pound green beans
2 shallots or green onions, chopped
1 tablespoon olive oil
1 clove garlic, minced

2 teaspoons fresh chopped tarragon
*   or ½ teaspoon dried tarragon*
2 tablespoons minced parsley
Salt and pepper, to taste

Trim the ends from the beans and slice regular green beans lengthwise or leave French-style beans whole. Cook in boiling salted water until crisp tender, about 5 to 7 minutes; drain. Meanwhile, in a skillet, sauté shallots in oil with garlic until soft. Add beans, tarragon, parsley, and salt and pepper, to taste, and shake pan to coat well. Makes 4 servings.

Pickled Beets

These piquant beets are nice to have on hand for a salad accompaniment.

2 tablespoons sugar
½ teaspoon dry mustard
½ teaspoon salt
8 whole cloves
1 clove garlic, peeled and chopped

⅓ cup cider vinegar
¼ cup water
2 cups cooked sliced fresh beets
1 small sweet red onion, sliced and
*   separated into rings*

In a saucepan, combine the sugar, mustard, salt, cloves, garlic, vinegar, and water; bring to a boil and pour over the beets and onion rings. Cover and chill at least 1 day. Makes 4 servings.

   Hint: This dish may be prepared 4 to 5 days in advance and refrigerated.

Broccoli with Garlic and Prosciutto

Sautéed garlic and prosciutto lend flair to broccoli flowerets.

1 bunch broccoli
2 teaspoons olive oil

2 cloves garlic
4 slices prosciutto, cut in strips

Cut the broccoli into small flowerets and peel the thick stalks. Steam the broccoli over simmering water until crisp tender, about 10 to 12 minutes. Meanwhile, heat the oil in a skillet, add garlic and sauté until light golden; add prosciutto and heat through. Add the broccoli and heat, coating it with sauce. Makes 2 to 3 servings.

Vineyard Brussels Sprouts

Grapes and pistachios bring a festive touch to Brussels sprouts.

1 pound Brussels sprouts
1 tablespoon olive oil or butter
1 cup seedless red or green grapes
2 tablespoons dry white wine

Dash each salt, pepper, and
*   nutmeg*
3 tablespoons pistachios or slivered
*   toasted almonds*

Cook Brussels sprouts in boiling salted water until tender, about 5 to 7 minutes. Drain. Add oil or butter and heat, shaking pan to coat lightly. Add grapes, wine, salt, pepper, and nutmeg and heat through. Serve sprinkled with nuts. Makes 4 servings.

Cabbage Wedges with Fennel

A fast simmer of cabbage wedges in milk with fennel makes a healthy vegetable dish.

½ head green cabbage	1 teaspoon fennel seeds
¾ cup milk	Salt and pepper, to taste

Cut the cabbage into 4 wedges, trimming the core. Place in a saucepan with milk and fennel seeds. Cover and simmer 4 to 5 minutes or until cabbage is crisp tender. With a slotted spoon, transfer cabbage to plates and season with salt and pepper. Makes 2 servings.

Glazed Carrots Dijon

Dijon mustard and caramelized brown sugar enliven everyday carrots.

*3 to 4 large carrots, peeled and
    sliced on the diagonal*
1 tablespoon butter

1½ teaspoons Dijon mustard
1½ teaspoons brown sugar
Salt and pepper, to taste

Cook the carrots in a small amount of boiling salted water until tender, about 8 to 10 minutes; drain well. Add the butter, mustard, sugar, and salt and pepper and heat, stirring, to glaze. Makes 2 to 3 servings.

Whipped Carrots and Spuds

This duo of spuds and carrots is an excellent accompaniment to grilled lamb, beef, or chicken.

3 large carrots, peeled and diced
2 medium potatoes, peeled and cut
    in 1-inch cubes
1 tablespoon butter

2 tablespoons whipping cream or
    milk, approximately
Dash each salt, pepper, and
    freshly grated nutmeg

Cook the carrots and potatoes in boiling salted water until very tender, about 15 minutes. Drain. Place the vegetables in a food processor fitted with a steel blade and process with butter, cream, and seasonings. If necessary add a little more cream or milk to achieve desired fluffy consistency. Makes 4 servings.

Carrots and Sugar Snaps

The snapping crisp goodness of sugar snap peas and sliced carrots is an ideal accompaniment to many entrées.

*2 carrots, peeled and sliced
    diagonally*
2 green onions, chopped

*½ pound sugar snap peas or pea
    pods*
Salt and pepper, to taste

Place the carrots and onions in a microwave-safe dish and cover loosely with plastic wrap. Microwave on high for 3 minutes. Remove plastic wrap, top carrots and onions with snap peas, cover again with plastic wrap, and microwave on high for 40 seconds. Season with salt and pepper. If desired, add a sliver of butter. Makes 2 servings.

Carrots Orangerie

Orange concentrate and honey glaze carrots superbly and simply.

*4 medium carrots, peeled and
  sliced on the diagonal
2 tablespoons orange juice
  concentrate*

*1 teaspoon honey
1 tablespoon brandy or Cognac*

Cook the carrots in a small amount of boiling salted water for 8 to 10 minutes or until barely tender; drain. Add orange concentrate, honey, and brandy to the pan and heat 1 to 2 minutes, shaking pan, until carrots are glazed and slightly caramelized. Makes 2 servings.

Indian Eggplant

This brilliant combination is a long-time favorite from a lovely Indian woman. It is a tantalizing interplay of flavors, colors, and temperature.

1 small onion, finely chopped
1 teaspoon olive oil
¼ cup tomato paste
2 tomatoes, peeled, seeded, and
    diced
1 teaspoon chopped fresh ginger
    root

1 teaspoon sugar
Salt and pepper, to taste
1 small eggplant
Olive oil
1 cup plain low-fat yogurt

In a skillet, sauté the onion in the 1 teaspoon oil until soft and golden. Add tomato paste, tomatoes, ginger, sugar, and salt and pepper, to taste. Cover and simmer 20 minutes. Meanwhile, slice the eggplant 1 inch thick, brush lightly with oil, and place on a baking sheet. Cover with foil. Bake in a 425° oven for 20 to 30 minutes or until cooked through. Transfer the eggplant to a serving platter. Spoon on the chilled yogurt and top with hot tomato sauce, leaving a rim of yogurt showing. Makes 2 to 3 servings.

Braised Leeks

Leeks are excellent hot or cold when braised in chicken broth.

*6 small leeks or 1 large bunch
asparagus or 1 head fennel
1 cup chicken stock
1 tablespoon virgin olive oil*

*6 whole allspice
2 tablespoons chopped Italian
parsley*

Trim the root ends from the leeks, remove tough fibrous outer layers, and trim off the green leaves. Split lengthwise. Hold each section under running water and rinse well. Or trim ends from the asparagus and peel thick stalks with a vegetable peeler. Or separate fennel into stalks of even length, trimming the ends. Lay the leeks, asparagus, or fennel in a saucepan, add chicken stock, oil, and allspice and bring to a boil. Cover and simmer 10 to 15 minutes for leeks or fennel or 5 to 7 minutes for asparagus or until tender. Remove to a serving dish. Cook down juices until reduced by two-thirds and spoon over the vegetables. Sprinkle with parsley. Makes 2 servings.

Sherried Mushrooms

Glazed mushrooms enhance a range of grilled entrées such as chicken, fish, beef, lamb, or pork.

2 teaspoons olive oil or butter
1 clove garlic, minced
1 shallot, chopped
½ pound button mushrooms,
  sliced, or oyster mushrooms

1 teaspoon chopped fresh tarragon
  or ¼ teaspoon dried tarragon
¼ cup dry sherry
Salt and pepper, to taste
2 tablespoons chopped parsley

In a large frying pan, heat the oil and sauté the garlic, shallot, and mushrooms until glazed, about 1 to 2 minutes. Add the tarragon, sherry, and salt and pepper, and cook very quickly to reduce juices. Sprinkle with parsley and remove from pan. Makes 2 servings.

Roasted Red Onions

This is a simple, delicious way to cook onions. When halved and roasted, they caramelize, turning sweet and mellow.

2 red sweet onions (about 5 inches in diameter), halved
1 tablespoon olive oil
2 tablespoons red wine vinegar

¼ cup ruby port or sherry
Chopped Italian parsley, for garnish

Leave the skins on the onions and halve crosswise. Drizzle cut surfaces with oil and place onions, cut side down, in a baking dish. Bake in a pre-heated 400° oven for 50 minutes or until soft. Transfer the onions to a platter and keep warm. Stir the vinegar and wine into the pan drippings and scrape up any residue. Put the liquid in a small saucepan and boil down until juices are reduced to a glaze. Spoon over onions. Garnish with parsley. Makes 4 servings.

Petit Pea Soufflé

This pretty grass green soufflé makes an ideal accompaniment to grilled fish, roast chicken, or barbecued lamb.

1 package (10 ounces) frozen petit peas, barely cooked and drained
¾ cup plain yogurt
2 tablespoons chopped shallots
1 cup chopped fresh spinach leaves
2 teaspoons fresh tarragon or ½ teaspoon dried tarragon
2 tablespoons chopped parsley
2 eggs, separated

4 egg whites
Dash of salt and pepper
2 tablespoons cornstarch
2 tablespoons grated Parmesan cheese
½ pound pea pods or sugar snap peas (optional)
1 teaspoon olive oil (optional)

Place the peas in a blender or food processor fitted with the steel blade. Add the yogurt, shallots, spinach, tarragon, parsley, and egg yolks and purée until blended. In a mixing bowl, beat the 6 egg whites until foamy; add salt, pepper, and cornstarch and beat until stiff. Fold in pea purée. Turn into a greased 1½-quart soufflé dish. Sprinkle with cheese. Bake in a preheated 325° oven for 30 to 35 minutes or until puffed and set.

If desired, quickly sauté pea pods or sugar snaps in oil in a large skillet, cooking 1 minute or until heated through and bright green. Serve alongside spoonfuls of soufflé. Makes 6 servings.

Rosemary Potato Dollars

Crispy potato wafers are a wonderful adjunct to barbecued meats.

2 large russet or yellow potatoes
2 tablespoons unsalted butter
1 tablespoon fresh rosemary
 or ¾ teaspoon dried rosemary

1 clove garlic, minced
Salt and pepper, to taste

Peel the potatoes and slice them as thinly as possible; wash under cold running water and pat dry. Melt the butter with rosemary and garlic. Place potatoes in a baking pan, pour the butter over them, and mix to coat well. Then separate potatoes, barely overlapping them. Season with salt and pepper. Bake in a preheated 450° oven for 30 to 40 minutes or until cooked through and crispy. Makes 2 servings.

Potatoes and Mushrooms with Saffron

A Spanish discovery, this makes an excellent side dish to roast chicken, grilled meats, or fish.

1¼ cups chicken broth
8 strands saffron
2 teaspoons olive oil
2 large russet or yellow baking potatoes, thinly sliced

¼ pound button mushrooms or wild mushrooms, thinly sliced
Salt and pepper, to taste
2 tablespoons roasted pistachios or pine nuts

Place the broth and saffron in a small saucepan, bring to a boil and let it boil gently until reduced to about ¾ cup. Add olive oil. Arrange potatoes and mushrooms, overlapping slightly, in an oiled 9-inch round baking dish. Season with salt and pepper; pour the saffron broth over the vegetables. Sprinkle with nuts. Cover and bake in a preheated 425° oven for 20 minutes; remove cover and continue baking 20 minutes longer or until potatoes are tender. Makes 2 servings.

Note: For a variation, sprinkle ⅓ cup shredded Jarlsberg or Gruyère cheese over the top before adding nuts.

Hot Spinach Sesame

A lively sesame dressing lends pizzazz to spinach.

1 bunch spinach, stems removed
1 teaspoon cider vinegar
1 teaspoon low-sodium soy sauce
1 teaspoon sesame oil

½ teaspoon brown sugar
¼ teaspoon prepared hot mustard
2 teaspoons toasted sesame seeds
4 cherry tomatoes

Steam the spinach until just wilted and still bright green; drain well. Mix together the vinegar, soy sauce, oil, sugar, and mustard. Spoon spinach into 2 small individual bowls and top with the sauce. Sprinkle with sesame seeds. Cut each tomato like a blossom by cutting into wedges but not all the way through. Garnish each serving with tomato flowers. Makes 2 servings.

Spinach and Mushroom Filo Roll

Filo encases a fat roll of chopped spinach and mushrooms for a savory, golden-brown vegetable pastry.

1 large onion, finely chopped
1 bunch green onions, chopped
1 tablespoon olive oil
¼ pound mushrooms, chopped
1 bunch spinach, stems removed
¼ cup chopped parsley
⅛ teaspoon nutmeg
Salt and pepper, to taste

3 eggs, beaten
¼ cup shredded Parmesan cheese
¼ cup shredded Swiss or Jarlsberg
    cheese or low-fat Swiss cheese
5 sheets filo dough
2 tablespoons melted unsalted
    butter

In a large frying pan, sauté the onion and green onions in oil over moderate heat, cooking until limp. Add the mushrooms and cook until glazed. Add spinach and heat until barely wilted. Remove from heat and drain off any extra liquid. Let cool. Mix in the parsley, nutmeg, salt and pepper, eggs, and cheese.

Lay out 1 sheet of filo and brush it lightly with melted butter; cover with a second sheet, butter lightly, and repeat layering remaining sheets and buttering between. Spoon spinach mixture along a long side of filo; fold up the ends of the filo 1 inch and roll up the dough, encasing the spinach. Place seam side down on a lightly buttered pan. Bake in a preheated 375° oven for 30 to 40 minutes or until crispy and browned. Cut in 2-inch slices and serve warm. Makes 6 servings.

Confetti-Tossed Spaghetti Squash

Golden spaghetti squash resembles al dente pasta in this healthy dish which can also be served as a light entrée.

*1 spaghetti squash, about
    1½ pounds
¼ cup chopped pistachios
¼ cup basil leaves, cut into thin
    strips
¼ cup oil-packed sun-dried
    tomatoes, drained and chopped*

*1 tablespoon extra virgin olive oil
¼ cup shredded Monterey Jack or
    Mozzarella cheese
¼ cup shredded dry Monterey Jack
    or Romano cheese*

Pierce the squash several times with a fork. Place on a microwave-safe baking dish, cover lightly with plastic wrap, and microwave on high for 9 to 10 minutes or until squash is fork-tender. Turn squash over once during cooking. Remove from oven; set aside to cool slightly. Halve the squash lengthwise; remove seeds. Lift out spaghetti-like strands with a fork and place on 2 microwave-safe dinner plates. Sprinkle each serving with pistachios, basil, tomatoes, and oil and fluff with 2 forks to mix. Mix the cheeses and sprinkle over the squash. Microwave plates on high about 30 seconds to heat through. Serve immediately. Makes 2 servings.

Sunchokes and Seedless Grapes

The nutty bite of sunchokes (Jerusalem artichokes) and refreshing tang of grapes make a neat duo served hot.

½ pound sunchokes, unpeeled and scrubbed
2 teaspoons butter or olive oil
2 tablespoons whipping cream

⅔ cup seedless red or green grapes
Dash each freshly grated nutmeg and black pepper

Cook the sunchokes in boiling salted water until tender, about 15 to 20 minutes. Drain, cool slightly, peel, and slice thinly. Melt the butter in a large skillet, add the sunchokes, and sauté to coat lightly. Add cream, grapes, nutmeg, and pepper and boil, shaking pan, until juices are reduced to a glaze and grapes are heated through. Makes 2 servings.

Shredded Zucchini

When squash from the garden becomes a bit oversized, this is a fine way to cook it as the extra moisture is squeezed out first.

1½ pounds zucchini
2 teaspoons olive oil
2 green onions, chopped
¼ cup chopped Italian parsley

2 teaspoons fresh oregano or
  ½ teaspoon dried oregano
Salt and pepper, to taste

Trim the ends from the zucchini and shred it finely using a food processor fitted with the shredder attachment. Put zucchini on a tea towel and squeeze out the extra moisture. Heat a large skillet over medium high heat, add oil, and sauté onions 1 minute. Add zucchini, parsley, oregano, and salt and pepper. Sauté 2 minutes, stirring occasionally, or until crisp tender. Makes 4 servings.

Pickled Vegetables

A sprightly vinegar bath lends a crisp bite to vegetables. Prepare an assortment for a colorful array.

2 pounds assorted vegetables:
  carrots, zucchini, cauliflower,
  radishes, green peppers, and
  jicama

1 cup boiling water
⅓ cup white distilled vinegar
3 tablespoons sugar
1 teaspoon salt

Prepare the vegetables in bite-sized pieces by peeling and slicing carrots and trimming and slicing remaining vegetables. In a bowl stir together the water, vinegar, sugar, and salt. Add vegetables, cover, and refrigerate for several hours or overnight. Makes about 8 servings.

Creamy Polenta with Arugula

With the peppery bite of arugula, this polenta makes an excellent side dish to sausages, pork, or turkey.

2 cups milk
Salt and pepper, to taste
½ cup polenta or yellow cornmeal

¼ cup shredded Romano or
    Parmesan cheese
⅓ cup chopped arugula

Bring the milk to a boil in a saucepan and stir in salt, pepper, and the polenta in a steady stream, stirring constantly to avoid lumps. Simmer for 8 minutes stirring almost constantly, or until thickened and creamy. Add the cheese and heat until cheese melts. Turn out on a serving plate and sprinkle with arugula. Makes 4 servings.

Risotto with Two Mushrooms

Fresh and dried mushrooms permeate this risotto with lots of earthy flavor. In the Italian tradition, it is meant to be served in a generous portion.

1 ounce dried porcini mushrooms
1½ cups chicken broth
1 tablespoon unsalted butter
1 tablespoon olive oil
2 shallots, chopped
¾ cup Arborio rice
¼ pound fresh mushrooms,
* chopped*

½ cup dry white wine
¼ cup heavy cream
2 tablespoons freshly grated
* Parmesan cheese*
Chopped Italian parsley, for
* garnish*

In a bowl, cover dried mushrooms with 1 cup hot water and let soak 1 hour. Remove mushrooms from the liquid, chop coarsely, and reserve. Strain the liquid through a sieve lined with several layers of cheesecloth and reserve.

In a saucepan, bring the broth to a boil and keep it at a low simmer.

In another saucepan, heat the butter and oil over moderate heat, add the shallots and sauté until they are soft. Add the rice and cook, stirring constantly, until it turns translucent. Add ½ cup of the heated broth and stir until the liquid is absorbed. Add another ½ cup stock, stirring, and continue cooking 10 minutes. Add the chopped dried mushrooms, fresh mushrooms, and half of the wine. When the wine is absorbed, add the remaining wine and some of the mushroom liquid, ½ cup at a time. Continue cooking, stirring in the remaining mushroom liquid and heated broth, ¼ cup at a time, as needed. When the rice is almost al dente, add the cream and cook until creamy. Stir in cheese and spoon onto hot plates. Pass additional cheese at the table. Makes 2 generous servings.

Brown Rice with Golden Raisins

Oven baking is an easy way to cook brown rice. If you prepare a double batch, package and freeze the balance in a zip-lock plastic bag, then reheat the rice in a microwave.

1 cup brown rice or a gourmet
*   style rice such as Wehani*
¼ teaspoon salt
⅛ teaspoon allspice

⅛ teaspoon pepper
¼ cup golden raisins
2 cups boiling water

Place the rice, salt, allspice, pepper, and raisins in a greased baking dish. Pour the water over the rice, cover, and bake in a preheated 375° oven for 45 minutes or until rice is tender. Makes 4 servings.

Baked Wild Rice with Pecans

Serve this wild rice dish with roast chicken or grilled meats.

1 cup wild rice
Water
2 stalks celery, chopped
3 green onions or 1 small sweet
*   onion, chopped*
2 teaspoons olive oil

⅓ cup chopped Italian parsley
2½ cups chicken broth
½ teaspoon dried marjoram
½ teaspoon dried thyme
Salt and pepper, to taste
⅓ cup chopped pecans or pistachios

Place rice in a bowl, cover with water, and let stand 1 hour; drain. In an oven-proof saucepan, sauté the celery and onions in oil until limp. Add the parsley, rice, broth, marjoram, and thyme. Season with salt and pepper. Bring to a boil, cover, and bake in a 350° oven for 1 hour or until rice is cooked through. Remove cover, scatter nuts over the top, and heat through. Makes 4 to 6 servings.

Hint: If desired, make a day in advance and reheat. This also freezes well.

Spicy Couscous

Couscous cooks in minutes, making it a joy for the cook on the run.

1 small sweet onion, chopped
1 teaspoon olive oil
1 teaspoon chopped ginger root
¼ teaspoon allspice
¼ teaspoon cinnamon
8 saffron threads

1 cup chicken broth
½ cup fine cracked wheat for
  couscous
3 tablespoons currants
2 tablespoons chopped pistachios
  or slivered almonds

In a skillet over medium heat, sauté the onion in oil with ginger root, allspice, cinnamon, and saffron, stirring, until soft and glazed. Add stock and bring to a boil. Stir in cracked wheat and currants, cover, and remove from heat and let stand 10 minutes. Sprinkle with nuts. Makes 4 servings.

Breads

Aromatic homemade yeast bread is a beloved treat and quite achievable on a weekend. With a heavy-duty mixer on hand, most breads take just 3 to 3½ hours from start to finish and can even be mixed up as the cook prepares dinner on a weeknight.

Individual coffee cans speed the baking and form neat round loaves easy for slicing and toasting or for sandwiches. Among the savory breads, the Garlic and Rosemary Whole Wheat Rounds and Whole Wheat Pecan Herb Bread are particularly good accompaniments to a soup or barbecue meal. Among the sweet breads, the Danish Chocolate Almond Twist and Sticky Cinnamon Rolls are crowd pleasers for a family occasion or weekend brunch.

Yeast breads freeze beautifully, especially if slipped into a plastic bag just as soon as they are barely cooled to room temperature. Frozen this way they will retain a fresh-baked taste upon thawing.

Garlic and Rosemary Whole Wheat Rounds

Roasted garlic studs this wholesome whole wheat round for a savory loaf to accompany cheeses and meats. For an appetizer or first course, it is also excellent toasted and served spread with chèvre, topped with sun-dried tomatoes.

2 packages active dry yeast	*2½ teaspoons salt*
2½ cups warm water	*3 tablespoons honey*
2 cups stone-ground whole wheat	*4 tablespoons olive oil*
flour	*2 tablespoons fresh rosemary*
3 cups unbleached all-purpose	*6 cloves garlic*
flour (approximately)	

Sprinkle yeast into ½ cup warm water (approximately 105–110°) and let stand until proofed, about 10 minutes. In a large mixing bowl, combine the whole wheat flour, ½ cup of the all-purpose flour, and the salt. Add the remaining water, the honey, and 3 tablespoons of the olive oil, and mix well using a heavy-duty electric mixer or beat with a wooden spoon by hand. Mix in proofed yeast and 1 tablespoon of the rosemary. Stir in remaining flour, adding enough to make a soft dough. Knead with the dough hook for 10 minutes or turn out on a lightly floured board and knead by hand. Place in a bowl, cover, and let rise in a warm place until doubled in size, about 1½ hours.

Meanwhile, place the garlic in a small baking dish, rub it with about ½ teaspoon of the remaining oil, and bake in a preheated 325° oven for 30 minutes or until soft; peel and slice. Add remaining rosemary and oil, mixing lightly.

Punch down the dough and turn it out on a lightly floured board. Divide in half and shape into 2 round loaves, kneading out air bubbles. Place each dough round in a lightly greased 9-inch round baking dish. With a finger, poke about 6 to 8 holes around the outer edge of the top surface. Fill with garlic and herb mixture, dividing evenly. Cover and let rise until doubled. Brush with olive oil. Bake in a preheated 375° oven for 40 minutes or until golden brown and loaves sound hollow when thumped. Let cool 10 minutes, turn out on a rack and cool completely. Makes 2 loaves.

Whole Wheat Pecan Herb Bread

This wholesome all-purpose bread is ideal for sandwiches or toast. Serve it as an accompaniment to a soup or salad meal. Bake the loaves either in 1-pound coffee cans or 9-inch pie pans.

2 packages active dry yeast
½ cup lukewarm water
2 tablespoons brown sugar
3 tablespoons olive oil
2 teaspoons salt
3 cups whole wheat flour
3 cups all-purpose unbleached
*   flour*
2½ cups water

¼ cup oat bran
¼ cup wheat germ
Zest of 1 orange, julienned
Zest of 1 lemon, julienned
½ cup pecans or walnuts
½ cup chopped mixed herbs:
*   oregano, parsley, thyme, and*
*   rosemary*

In a small bowl, sprinkle the yeast into the lukewarm water, add a pinch of sugar, and let stand until dissolved and proofed. In a mixing bowl, combine the brown sugar, oil, salt, 1 cup whole wheat flour, and 1 cup unbleached flour. Gradually add the remaining water. Mix in the yeast, oat bran, wheat germ, and citrus peels. Gradually add enough flour to make a soft dough. Mix in the nuts and herbs. Knead with the dough hook of a heavy-duty mixer or turn out on a board and knead lightly for 10 minutes. Place in a bowl, cover with plastic wrap, and let rise in a warm place until doubled in size.

Punch dough down, turn out on a board, and shape into four balls. Insert in 4 greased 1-pound coffee cans or 9-inch pie pans. Cover and let rise until doubled. Bake in a preheated 375° oven for 30 to 35 minutes or until golden brown. Turn breads out of cans and let cool on a rack. Makes 4 loaves.

Grammy's Four Grain Bread

The flours may vary in this wholesome bread. If barley flour is unavailable substitute whole wheat.

2½ cups warm water
1 cup old-fashioned oatmeal
2 packages active dry yeast
Zest of 1 orange, julienned
2½ teaspoons salt
⅓ cup canola oil or butter

¼ cup dark molasses
1 cup milk
1½ cups barley flour
1 cup rye flour
3 cups bread flour or unbleached
  flour

Place 2 cups of the water and the oatmeal in a saucepan and bring to a boil. Boil 1 minute, then turn into a mixing bowl; let cool to lukewarm. Sprinkle yeast into the remaining ½ cup warm water and let stand until dissolved. Add the orange zest, yeast, salt, oil, and molasses to the oatmeal mixture. Heat the milk until warm and stir it into the oatmeal mixture. Gradually add the barley, rye, and bread flours, mixing to make a soft dough.

Turn out on a lightly floured board and knead until smooth and elastic. Place in a bowl, grease top lightly, cover, and let rise in a warm place until doubled in size. Turn the dough out of the bowl, punch down, and knead to remove air bubbles. Divide into three parts and shape into loaves. Place in 3 greased 9 by 5-inch loaf pans or shape into round loaves and place on greased baking sheets. Cover and let rise until doubled in size. Bake in a preheated 375° oven for 35 to 40 minutes, or until the loaves sound hollow when thumped. Makes 3 loaves.

Cinnamon Wheat Germ Rounds

Baked in coffee cans, these wholesome loaves slice easily for neat sand-wiches or toast.

2 packages active dry yeast
½ cup lukewarm water
½ cup unbleached flour
Pinch sugar
¼ cup honey
3 tablespoons canola or safflower
   oil
2 teaspoons salt

1 teaspoon cinnamon
Julienned zest of 2 oranges
3 cups whole wheat flour
3 cups unbleached flour
   (approximately)
⅓ cup wheat germ
2½ cups warm water

In a small bowl, sprinkle yeast into the ½ cup lukewarm water, stir in ½ cup unbleached flour and a pinch sugar. Cover and let rise for 10 to 15 minutes or until tripled in size. In a mixing bowl, combine the honey, oil, salt, cinnamon, orange zest, 2 cups whole wheat flour, 1 cup un-bleached flour, and wheat germ. Gradually pour in the remaining 2½ cups water and beat until smooth. Add the proofed yeast, mixing well. Gradually add remaining whole wheat and unbleached flours, adding enough to make a soft dough. Insert dough hook in a heavy-duty mixer or turn out on a floured board and knead by hand for 5 to 10 minutes. Place in a bowl, cover with a towel, and let rise in a warm place until doubled in size.

Punch dough down, divide into quarters, and shape into balls. Place balls in 4 greased 1-pound coffee cans or 4 9-inch pie pans. Bake in a pre-heated 375° oven for 35 to 40 minutes or until loaves sound hollow when thumped. Let cool 5 minutes, then remove from cans. Makes 4 loaves.

Hint: When cool, slip loaves into plastic bags, tie securely, and freeze up to three weeks.

Brioche Cheese Braid

This golden cheese bread makes a meal with a soup, a salad, or a sliced meat terrine. It is best served warm to release the buttery flavor and make the texture springy.

1 package active dry yeast
¼ cup lukewarm water
½ cup milk
6 tablespoons butter or margarine
2 tablespoons sugar
½ teaspoon salt
3 eggs

1 egg, separated
3¼ cups unbleached flour
*   (approximately)*
1½ cups diced or shredded
*   Jarlsberg, Gruyère, or*
*   Swiss-style cheese*

Sprinkle yeast into lukewarm water and stir until dissolved. Heat milk until lukewarm. In a large bowl, beat the butter until creamy and add sugar, salt, whole eggs, and egg yolk, beating well. Add milk and yeast mixture. Gradually add just enough flour to make a soft dough, beating well after each addition. Turn out on a lightly floured board. Knead until smooth and satiny. Place in a greased bowl. Cover and let rise in a warm place until doubled in size.

Turn out on a lightly floured board and knead cheese into the dough. Divide into three pieces. Roll into ropes about 14 inches long. Braid dough on a greased baking sheet. Cover and let rise in a warm place until doubled in size. Brush with lightly beaten egg white to make a glaze. Bake in a preheated 350° oven for 30 to 35 minutes or until golden brown and loaf sounds hollow when thumped. Makes 1 large loaf.

Orange Marmalade Coffee Can Breads

Orange zest and marmalade enhance these coffee can loaves of bread that are especially easy and attractive to slice.

2 packages active dry yeast
½ cup lukewarm water
6 to 7½ cups unbleached flour
Pinch sugar
4 eggs
⅓ cup orange marmalade

⅓ cup canola oil
1½ teaspoons salt
¼ teaspoon ground nutmeg
Zest of 2 oranges, julienned
1 cup milk, heated to lukewarm
1 cup orange juice

Sprinkle the yeast into warm water, stir lightly, add ½ cup of flour and the sugar, and let stand until proofed and triple in volume, about 20 minutes. In a large mixing bowl, place eggs, marmalade, oil, salt, nutmeg, and orange zest. Mix until blended. Add the milk and orange juice. Add 2 cups of the flour and beat until smooth. Add the yeast sponge and mix well. Gradually add remaining flour, adding enough to make a soft dough. Beat with a dough hook 10 minutes or turn out on a floured board and knead 10 minutes. Place in a lightly greased bowl, cover, and let rise in a warm place until doubled in size, about 1½ hours.

Punch dough down, turn out on a floured board, and knead lightly to release air bubbles. Divide the dough into 6 equal pieces. Shape into 6 round loaves. Place in greased 1-pound coffee cans. Cover and let rise until dough almost fills the cans. Bake in a preheated 375° oven for 30 minutes or until golden brown. If tops become golden brown early in the baking process, cover with a loose sheet of foil to continue baking. Remove and let cool on racks. Makes 6 loaves.

Golden Raisin and Almond Rounds

This aromatic sweet bread is excellent for breakfast, or toast it and spread with Yogurt Cheese and raspberry jelly for a special treat.

Sponge:

1 package active dry yeast
½ cup lukewarm water

½ cup flour
Pinch sugar

Dough:

1 package active dry yeast
½ cup lukewarm water
⅔ cup sugar
Grated zest of 2 oranges
Grated zest of 2 lemons
1 teaspoon vanilla extract
¼ teaspoon nutmeg
4 eggs or 3 eggs and 2 yolks

8 tablespoons (1 stick) butter or
   margarine
1 cup milk, heated to lukewarm
1 teaspoon salt
5 to 6 cups unbleached flour
1¼ cups golden raisins
½ cup slivered almonds

Almond Paste Topping: (optional)

½ cup blanched almonds
½ cup sugar

2 egg whites

Prepare sponge. In a small bowl sprinkle 1 package yeast into the ½ cup water and stir in the ½ cup flour and a pinch of sugar. Cover with plastic wrap and let stand in a warm place for 20 to 30 minutes or until bubbly and doubled in volume.

For the dough, sprinkle 1 package yeast into ½ cup warm water in a large mixing bowl and let stand until creamy, about 10 minutes. Add the sponge and beat thoroughly. Add the sugar, grated orange and lemon zest, vanilla extract, nutmeg, and eggs and beat well. Add the butter, milk, salt, and 2 cups flour and mix thoroughly. Gradually add 2 more cups flour and mix well using a heavy-duty mixer. Then add enough remaining flour to make a soft dough. Mix in the raisins and the ½ cup almonds. Turn out on a floured board and knead lightly. Place in a bowl, cover, and let rise in a warm place until doubled in size, about 1½ hours.

Turn out on a floured board and knead lightly. Divide in half. Shape into 2 round loaves and place in greased 2-quart soufflé dishes or charlotte molds. Or place in 5 greased 1-pound coffee tins. Cover and let rise until doubled, about 45 minutes.

Meanwhile, prepare the Almond Paste Topping. In a food processor fitted with a steel blade, grind almonds finely. Add sugar and blend. Add egg white and mix to blend. Mixture will be runny. Spread on the top of the dough rounds. Place in a preheated 400° oven. Immediately turn temperature down to 375° and bake for 20 minutes. Reduce temperature to 350° and bake 20 to 25 minutes longer. If tops brown too quickly, cover with a sheet of foil. Let cool on racks 10 minutes, then remove from pans. Makes 2 large loaves or 5 coffee can loaves.

Featherlight Lemon Anise Rounds

Lemon zest and anise seed flavor these light round loaves of bread. Slice and toast it or enjoy it in a sandwich with sliced turkey or chicken.

2 packages active dry yeast
½ cups lukewarm water
3 eggs
¼ cup honey
¼ cup canola or olive oil
1½ teaspoons salt

1 tablespoon anise seed
Zest of 2 lemons, julienned
1 cup milk, heated to lukewarm
¾ cup lukewarm water
5 to 5½ cups unbleached flour

Sprinkle yeast into ½ cup of the warm water, stir lightly, and let stand until proofed, about 10 minutes. Place the eggs, honey, oil, salt, anise seed, and lemon zest in a large mixing bowl and mix until blended. Add the milk and the remaining ¾ cup of warm water. Add 2 cups of the flour and beat until smooth. Add dissolved yeast and mix well. Gradually add remaining flour, adding enough to make a soft dough. Beat with a dough hook 10 minutes or turn out on a floured board and knead 10 minutes. Place in a lightly greased bowl, cover, and let rise in a warm place until doubled in size, about 1½ hours.

Punch dough down, turn out on a floured board, and knead lightly to release air bubbles. Divide the dough into four equal pieces and shape into four round loaves. Place on greased 9-inch pie pans. Cover and let rise until doubled in size. Bake in a preheated 375° oven for 30 to 35 minutes or until golden brown. Remove and let cool on racks. Makes 4 loaves.

Dried Fruit Almond Variation: Add 1¼ cups snipped dried apricots or golden raisins and ¾ cup slivered blanched almonds to the dough after incorporating the flour, and let rise.

Mom's Sticky Cinnamon Rolls

This is a sweet roll to delight any age. If desired, pecans may enhance the sticky caramel coating each swirled roll.

2 packages active dry yeast
½ cup lukewarm water
1 cup milk
6 tablespoons butter
½ cup sugar
1 teaspoon salt
1 teaspoon vanilla extract

3 eggs
5 cups all-purpose flour
Melted butter
Cinnamon
⅔ cup light brown sugar
Sticky Caramel (recipe follows)

Sprinkle the yeast into the lukewarm water and let stand until dissolved. Heat the milk and butter together until butter melts. Pour into a large mixing bowl. Stir in the sugar, salt, and vanilla extract; cool to lukewarm. Stir in yeast mixture. Add eggs, one at a time, and beat until smooth. Gradually beat in enough flour to make a soft dough. Turn out on a floured board and knead until smooth and satiny. Place in a greased bowl. Cover and let rise in a warm place until doubled in size, about 1½ hours.

Divide dough in half and knead lightly. Roll each piece into a 10 by 12-inch rectangle. Spread with melted butter and sprinkle lightly with cinnamon. Scatter ⅓ cup brown sugar onto each rectangle. Roll up. Cut into ¾-inch slices. Place in prepared caramel-coated pans (see below). Cover and let rise until doubled in size. Bake in a preheated 350° oven for 30 minutes or until golden brown. Immediately turn upside down on racks and lift off pans. Serve warm or cool. Makes about 3 dozen rolls.

STICKY CARAMEL:

Select two 9 by 13-inch baking pans. Place 2½ tablespoons butter, ¼ cup light corn syrup, and ⅔ cup firmly packed light brown sugar in each pan. Heat in a preheated 350° oven just until butter melts and mixture bubbles. Spread coating evenly over bottom of pans. If desired, scatter ⅓ cup pecan or walnut halves onto each caramel-coated pan. Let cool slightly to room temperature before topping with cinnamon dough slices as directed.

Danish Chocolate Almond Twist

This decorative loaf is a winner for a special brunch or coffee time treat. Make in advance and freeze.

Sponge:

1 package active dry yeast	Pinch sugar
½ cup warm water	½ cup flour

Dough:

1 package active dry yeast	3 eggs
¼ cup water	4½ to 5 cups unbleached flour
6 tablespoons sugar	(approximately)
6 tablespoons butter or margarine	1 cup warm milk
1 teaspoon salt	1 egg white, beaten until foamy
2 teaspoons vanilla extract or	3 tablespoons sliced almonds
½ teaspoon ground cardamom	Chocolate Streusel (recipe follows)

First prepare the sponge. In a small bowl, sprinkle 1 package yeast into lukewarm water. Add pinch of sugar and beat in the ½ cup flour. Cover with plastic wrap and let stand 20 to 30 minutes or until doubled in size.

In a large mixing bowl, sprinkle the remaining 1 package yeast into the ¼ cup lukewarm water and stir until blended; let stand until creamy, about 10 minutes. Add the sponge and beat until smooth. Add the sugar, butter, salt, vanilla extract, and eggs and beat well. Add 1 cup flour and beat until smooth. Add milk and gradually add 2 cups more flour, beating well. Gradually add remaining flour, adding enough to make a soft dough. Turn out on a floured board and knead lightly. Place in a bowl, cover, and let rise in a warm place until doubled in size, about 1½ hours. Punch dough down, turn out on a board, and knead lightly.

Cut the dough in half. Roll one half into a 10 by 4-inch rectangle. Sprinkle with half the Chocolate Streusel. Roll up and place seam side down on a buttered baking sheet. Repeat with remaining dough and filling. Cut through the rolls to within ½ inch of bottom at ¾-inch intervals. Starting at one end, pull and twist each slice to lay flat, alternately on opposite sides. Cover with a towel and let rise in a warm place until doubled, about 45 minutes. Brush loaves with egg white and sprinkle with nuts. Place in a preheated 350° oven, reduce heat to 325° and bake for 30 to 35 minutes or until golden brown. Makes 2 loaves.

CHOCOLATE STREUSEL:

½ cup sugar
3 tablespoons flour
2 tablespoons cocoa

½ teaspoon cinnamon
2 tablespoons soft butter

In a small bowl, mix together the sugar, flour, cocoa, and cinnamon. Cut in the butter until the mixture resembles fine crumbs.

Persimmon Tea Loaves

A surplus of persimmons from the garden inspires this fast tea bread that freezes well. Slice it thinly and spread with Yogurt Cheese or cream cheese.

1 cup sugar
1 cup plus 2 tablespoons flour
1 teaspoon soda
¼ teaspoon salt
1 teaspoon baking powder
1 teaspoon cinnamon

1 egg
1 teaspoon vanilla extract
¼ cup milk
1 cup persimmon pulp
1 tablespoon melted butter
½ cup chopped walnuts

Place the sugar, flour, soda, salt, baking powder, and cinnamon in a bowl and mix well. In another bowl, beat the egg and stir in the vanilla extract, milk, persimmon pulp, and butter. Add the dry ingredients to the liquid ingredients and beat well. Mix in the nuts. Spoon the batter into 2 greased and floured small 3½ by 7½-inch loaf pans. Cover with foil and bake in a preheated 350° oven for 45 to 50 minutes or until a toothpick inserted comes out clean. Uncover and cool before removing from pan. Makes 2 small loaves.

Healthy Yogurt Muffins

These muffins are chock full of healthy ingredients. If desired, keep batter covered in the refrigerator and use as needed for fresh-baked muffins. The batter keeps 10 days to 2 weeks. The recipe may also be doubled with ease.

½ cup rolled oats
2 tablespoons oat bran
½ cup boiling water
⅓ cup brown sugar, packed
2 tablespoons honey
2 tablespoons canola or olive oil
1 egg
1 cup nonfat or low-fat yogurt
1½ teaspoons baking soda

½ teaspoon salt
½ cup whole wheat flour
½ cup unbleached all-purpose flour
1 cup bran cereal
½ cup golden or dark raisins or snipped dried apricots
⅓ cup chopped walnuts or pecans

Place the oats and oat bran in a mixing bowl and pour the water over them. Mix in the sugar, honey, oil, egg, and yogurt. In another bowl stir together the baking soda, salt, flours, and bran cereal and mix lightly into the bran mixture. Stir in the raisins and nuts. Spoon into paper-lined muffin tins. Bake in a preheated 375° oven for 15 to 20 minutes or until golden brown. Makes 16 muffins.

Desserts

The working cook can rely on fresh fruit, cookies, and freezer treats such as frozen yogurt, ice cream, and sherbet for instant weekday sweets. White Chocolate and Pistachio Chipperoos, Biscotti, Chocolate Almond Wafers, and Golden Raisin Rum Brownies are delicious for the lunch bag or snacking as well as a dinnertime dessert. Baked on the weekend, the cookies stay fresh in a tin or the freezer. Warm them slightly in the oven before serving so they'll seem like just baked.

For special guest occasions or weekend indulging, the Lemon Cheese Tart is a seasonal spectacular topped with fresh berries. Let Basque Chocolate Mousse please the calorie counter. Honey Ice Cream and Grand Marnier Ice Cream are luscious mated with fresh berries, and Frozen Lemon Shells or White Chocolate Parfait can frostily await any occasion.

For the family birthday, the Chocolate Angel Cake, Feathery Chocolate Almond Cake, or Chocolate Almond Torte will please the fancy of any chocoholic.

Papaya Fruit Plate

An ornamental arrangement of multi-colored fruits is easy to assemble and makes an enticing and refreshing climax to dinner.

1 papaya   *1 cup large strawberries*
2 kiwi fruit   *1 lime*

Peel, halve, and seed the papaya and cut into strips. Peel and thinly slice kiwi fruit. On 4 dessert plates arrange a few slices of papaya overlapped with 2 or 3 slices of kiwi fruit. Place berries in a cluster and garnish with lime wedges. Makes 4 servings.

Berries with Cassis

A splash of cassis turns berries into an instant dessert.

2 cups strawberries, halved or sliced
1 cup blueberries
⅓ cup cassis syrup or crème de
*   cassis liqueur*

Frozen vanilla yogurt or crème
*   fraîche, for garnish*

Gently mix the strawberries and blueberries in a bowl and spoon the cassis over them. Spoon into serving dishes and top with a dollop of frozen yogurt or crème fraîche. Makes 4 servings.

Snow Peaches
with Raspberry Sauce

The brilliance of raspberry purée on summer peaches or nectarines makes a magnificent dessert. If white peaches or nectarines are not available, use yellow ones for a more brilliant coloration.

1 package (10 ounces) frozen rasp-berries, thawed, juice reserved
1 tablespoon framboise liqueur or eau de vie

4 white Babcock peaches or white nectarines
3 tablespoons pistachios

Purée the raspberries with their juice in a blender and push through a wire strainer to remove seeds. Stir in the liqueur. Peel and slice peaches and place in dessert bowls. Pour the berry purée over the peaches and sprinkle with nuts. Makes 4 servings.

Rhubarb and Strawberry Bowls

The fresh tang of raw rhubarb is a wonderful accent with berries for a light dessert. It is a favorite from the Ferme St. Simeon country restaurant in Honfleur, France.

*2 stalks rhubarb, finely diced
   (about ⅔ cup)
2 cups strawberries, sliced*

*2 tablespoons honey
1 teaspoon grated lemon peel
Vanilla bean ice cream, for garnish*

In a bowl, combine the rhubarb, berries, honey, and lemon peel. Let stand 1 hour for juices to blend. Serve in dessert bowls topped with a scoop of ice cream. Makes 4 servings.

Strawberries in Red Wine

Berries and wine mate in this classic French dessert. Serve in burgundy glasses for a festive presentation.

1½ pints strawberries
¼ cup sugar

1½ cups dry red wine such as
Zinfandel or Gamay Beaujolais

Wash and hull the strawberries. Alternate layers of berries and sugar in a wide-mouthed tall cylindrical jar or glass serving container. Pour enough wine over the strawberries to cover them. Let stand at room temperature at least 3 hours. Makes 4 servings.

Ruby Fruit Compote

As this compote chills, the berries exude their ruby juices, turning the citrus syrup scarlet.

Juice and grated zest of 1 orange   *1½ cups strawberries*
Juice and grated zest of 1 lime   *½ cup raspberries*
¼ cup sugar   *1 cup seedless red grapes*
2 cups watermelon balls   *Mint sprigs, for garnish*

In a saucepan, combine the orange juice, lime juice, citrus peels, and sugar. Bring to a boil and cook until sugar is dissolved, stirring constantly. Remove from heat, cool, and chill.

Place the watermelon, strawberries, raspberries, and grapes in a bowl. Pour the syrup over the fruit. Cover and chill 2 to 3 hours or longer, stirring gently once or twice. Serve in dessert bowls and garnish with mint. Makes 4 to 6 servings.

Caramel Cookie Baskets with Berries and Sherbet

Crispy caramel cookies hold sherbet and berries for a fetching dessert treat to delight family or guests.

2 tablespoons margarine, melted
3 tablespoons brown sugar, packed
2 tablespoons all-purpose flour
1/8 teaspoon almond extract
1 egg white
1 tablespoon finely chopped
    pistachios

1 pint raspberry sherbet or frozen
    berry yogurt
2 cups raspberries and blueberries,
    mixed
1 tablespoon framboise (optional)

In a bowl, place the margarine, sugar, flour, almond extract, and egg white, and mix until blended. On a non-stick baking sheet, spoon out a generous tablespoon of batter and spread to make a 5- or 6-inch circle. Repeat, placing 2 cookies on each baking sheet. Sprinkle with nuts. Bake in a preheated 350° oven for 6 to 7 minutes or until edges are golden brown. With a thin spatula, remove cookies from the sheet at once and drape them over the back side of a custard cup, shaping each cookie to form a cup. Let cool until set. If made in advance, store the cookies in a tin. To serve, arrange cookies on dessert plates and add a scoop of sherbet. Toss the berries with framboise, if desired, and spoon them over the sherbet. Makes 4 servings.

Winter Pears Helene

Juicy sliced winter pears, frosty ice cream, and hot fudge sauce make an appealing dessert combination.

4 ounces semisweet chocolate
  (⅔ cup chocolate bits)
⅓ cup light cream or half-and-half
3 tablespoons light corn syrup
½ teaspoon vanilla extract

2 large Comice pears
1 pint vanilla or toasted almond
  ice cream
¼ cup toasted chopped almonds
  (optional)

Melt the chocolate, cream, and corn syrup in the top of a double boiler over hot water, stirring the mixture until smoothly blended. Stir in the vanilla extract. When ready to serve, halve, core, and slice the pears and arrange in dessert bowls. Top each serving with a scoop of ice cream and spoon hot fudge sauce over it. If desired, sprinkle with nuts. Makes 4 servings.

Chocolate-Dipped Strawberries

Dark chocolate-dipped berries tantalize the eye and taste buds in this winsome dessert. The white chocolate variation is equally tempting.

4 ounces semisweet chocolate
1 tablespoon orange liqueur

2 tablespoons coffee
3 cups strawberries with stems,
   chilled

Melt the chocolate with the liqueur and coffee in a double boiler over hot, not boiling, water. Stir to blend. Dip the berries halfway into the chocolate to coat. Place on a foil-lined pan, stem down, or in paper candy cups, and chill until chocolate sets. Serve on plates lined with grape or citrus leaves, if available. Makes 4 servings.

White Chocolate Variation: Substitute 4 ounces white chocolate for semisweet chocolate, 2 tablespoons milk for coffee, and if desired, substitute 1 tablespoon framboise liqueur for the orange liqueur.

Stuffed Apricots
with Honey Gingered Cheese

Fresh apricots hold a creamy ginger cheese for a quick and easy, pretty dessert plate.

12 apricots
1 cup low-fat ricotta cheese
3 tablespoons honey
2 tablespoons orange-flavored
*   liqueur*

2 ounces candied ginger, finely
*   chopped (about ⅓ cup)*
Edible blossoms, if desired, or
*   mint sprigs*

Halve and pit the apricots. In a bowl, stir together the ricotta cheese, honey, liqueur, and ginger. Spoon cheese mixture inside each apricot half. Arrange on dessert plates. Garnish with a blossom, if desired. Makes 4 servings.

Brandied Apple Slices

Hot apple slices intensify in flavor with this easy cloaking of lemon, liqueur, sugar, and egg.

*3 Granny Smith or Golden
   Delicious apples*
Juice of ½ lemon
1 egg
1 tablespoon sugar
2 teaspoons cornstarch

*2 tablespoons brandy, Calvados,
   Amaretto, or orange liqueur*
Powdered sugar
*Ice cream or frozen yogurt for
   accompaniment*

Peel, core, and slice the apples thinly. Place in a bowl and toss with the lemon juice. In a small bowl, whisk the egg, sugar, cornstarch, and brandy together, pour over the apples, and mix well. Turn into a buttered 9-inch pie pan or baking dish. Bake in a preheated 375° oven for 45 minutes or until apples are golden brown and puffy. Remove from oven, sprinkle with powdered sugar, and serve accompanied by a scoop of ice cream or frozen yogurt. Makes 2 to 3 servings.

Frozen Lemon Shells

Hollow out lemon shells for a charming container to hold Lemon Ice or frozen yogurt for an eye-catching, make-ahead dessert.

4 large lemons
1 pint Lemon Ice (see page 212) or
    peach frozen yogurt

Slice off the tops of the lemons one-third of the way down. Slice off just enough of the other end to make a firm base for the shell to stand upright. Squeeze the juice from the fruit, saving the juice for another purpose and keeping the shells intact. Remove any remaining membrane, being careful not to cut the shells. Pack each shell with frozen yogurt. Top with lemon peel caps and freeze, covered, until firm. Serve on plates lined with lemon leaves, if available. Makes 4 servings.

Lemon Ice

This wonderfully refreshing ice is excellent tucked inside hollow lemon shells or serve it with assorted small scoops of raspberry sherbet and vanilla frozen yogurt. Another time try it with limes.

½ cup plus ½ teaspoon sugar   *2 teaspoons grated lemon zest*
¾ cup water   *6 tablespoons lemon juice*

Combine the ½ cup of sugar and water in a saucepan and bring to a boil, stirring to dissolve the sugar. Cook until syrup is clear. Mash lemon zest with remaining sugar to bring out its oils. Remove syrup from heat and stir in lemon zest and juice. Let cool and chill thoroughly. Pour into a shallow pan, cover, and freeze until solid. Scoop into the container of a food processor and process until light and fluffy. Return to a freezer container, cover, and freeze until firm. Makes about 1 pint.

Iced Coffee Floats

A popular Italian café drink makes a delicious dessert treat for a hot summery day. Use decaffeinated brewed coffee, if desired.

½ pint vanilla or coffee ice cream
2 cups hot brewed coffee

Scoop the ice cream into heat-proof glasses. Pour hot coffee over it and serve at once. Makes 2 servings.

Honey Ice Cream

This creamy ice cream is superb alone or enhance it with fresh straw-berries, raspberries, or sliced nectarines or peaches.

4 egg yolks
¾ cup honey
2 cups (1 pint) half-and-half

2 teaspoons grated orange zest
2 cups whipping cream

Beat the egg yolks slightly in the top pan of a double boiler and stir in honey, half-and-half, and orange peel. Place over simmering water and cook, stirring constantly, until mixture is custard-like and coats the spoon. Remove from heat and place over a pan of ice cold water to chill immediately. Refrigerate until cold, or for several hours if possible. Stir in the cream. Pour into a 2-quart ice cream maker. Freeze according to manufacturer's directions. Serve at once or freeze to hold until serving time. Makes about 1¾ quarts.

Grand Marnier Ice Cream, Italian Style

In the Italian fashion, this method gives an ultra-creamy consistency to ice cream.

¾ cup plus 2 teaspoons sugar
1 tablespoon light corn syrup
¼ cup water
5 egg yolks

2 teaspoons freshly grated orange
 zest
2 cups whipping cream
1¾ cups half-and-half
¼ cup Grand Marnier

Combine the ¾ cup sugar, corn syrup, and water in a small pan. Bring to a boil and boil until the temperature reaches 238° on a candy thermometer or soft-ball stage.

Meanwhile, beat the egg yolks with an electric mixer until thick and pale yellow. Continuing beating the yolks and slowly pour in the sugar syrup in a fine, steady stream. Beat until the mixture cools to room temperature, about 7 minutes. When cool, refrigerate mixture until cold, or for several hours if possible. Mash the orange zest with 2 teaspoons sugar to bring out its oils and stir into chilled mixture with the whipping cream, half-and-half, and Grand Marnier. Pour into a 2-quart ice cream freezer. Freeze according to manufacturer's directions until ice cream is frozen. Makes about 1¾ quarts.

White Chocolate Parfait

Freeze this silken parfait ahead, ready to top with berries or sprinkle with pistachios or toasted almonds at serving time.

6 egg yolks
½ cup sugar
1 cup milk
6 ounces white chocolate chips
1 teaspoon grated orange peel

1 cup heavy cream
Raspberries, strawberries,
    pistachios, or toasted almonds,
    for garnish, if desired

In the top of a double boiler, beat the egg yolks and sugar until thick and light in color. Whisk in the milk. Place over hot water and whisk until triple in volume. Remove from heat and add chocolate, stirring until blended. Cool over a pan of ice water. Whip cream until stiff and fold into the chocolate mixture. Spoon into soufflé dishes or small glass bowls, cover, and freeze until firm. To serve, top with raspberries, strawberries, or nuts, if desired. Makes 6 servings.

Hint: The parfait may be frozen for 2 to 3 weeks.

Basque Chocolate Mousse

Coffee and orange flavors blend with chocolate in this ambrosial mousse.

4 ounces (⅔ cup) semisweet
chocolate bits
2 tablespoons strong coffee
2 tablespoons Cointreau or other
orange liqueur
4 eggs, separated
1 teaspoon vanilla extract

1 tablespoon sugar
2 tablespoons chopped roasted
pistachios or toasted slivered
almonds
Whipped cream for garnish
(optional)

Place the chocolate bits and coffee in a small pan over simmering water and heat until melted, stirring to blend. Remove from heat and stir in liqueur. Mix in egg yolks, one at a time. Stir in vanilla extract. Beat the egg whites until soft peaks form, then add the sugar, beating until stiff but not dry. Stir one-third of the whites into the chocolate mixture, then fold in the remaining whites. Turn into 4 dessert bowls, parfait glasses, or wine glasses. Cover and chill until set, about 2 hours. At serving time, sprinkle with toasted nuts and top with whipped cream, if desired. Makes 4 servings.

Zabaglione with Berries

For an impromptu dessert, serve Zabaglione hot, or make ahead if there is time since it is excellent chilled. This recipe is a favorite from an Italian neighbor of years ago.

4 egg yolks
¼ cup sugar
⅓ cup sweet white dessert wine

1 teaspoon grated lemon zest
2 cups raspberries, blueberries, or
    strawberries, sliced

In the top of a double boiler, beat the egg yolks until light, then beat in the sugar, wine, and lemon zest. Over simmering water, beat with a wire whip or portable electric beater until it triples in volume and retains a peak, about 7 minutes. If desired, cool immediately by placing the pan in ice water, then chill. Or serve hot. Using tall, slender glasses, alternate spoonfuls of Zabaglione and berries. Makes 4 servings.

Lemon Soufflé Custard

A soufflé topping caps this tart custard pudding.

3 tablespoons flour
½ cup sugar
3 eggs, separated
¼ teaspoon salt
¼ teaspoon cream of tartar

2 tablespoons melted butter
1½ teaspoons grated lemon zest
⅓ cup lemon juice
1 cup milk

In a small bowl, mix together the flour and ¼ cup of the sugar. Beat egg whites until foamy. Add the salt and cream of tartar and beat until stiff but not dry; beat in the remaining ¼ cup sugar. Beat the egg yolks until thick, then add the sugar–flour mixture, melted butter, grated lemon zest, lemon juice, and milk. Fold egg white meringue into the egg yolk mixture. Spoon into 4 buttered individual soufflé dishes or other small baking dishes. Place in a pan containing 1 inch of hot water and bake in a preheated 350° oven for 20 to 25 minutes, or until set. Makes 4 servings.

Hint: Make a day in advance and serve chilled, if desired.

White Chocolate Soufflé with Raspberry Sauce

Scarlet raspberry sauce gilds this creamy pale chocolate soufflé for a delectable pairing of flavors. For maximum crustiness, bake the soufflé in a large round or oval baking dish, such as a copper au gratin pan.

6 ounces white chocolate bits
6 eggs, separated
¼ teaspoon salt
¼ teaspoon cream of tartar
¾ cup sugar

1 teaspoon vanilla extract or
1 tablespoon framboise
1 package (12 ounces) frozen
raspberries, thawed

Heat the chocolate in a small bowl over hot water until melted; let cool slightly. Beat egg whites until foamy, add salt and cream of tartar and beat until soft peaks form. Add ¼ cup of the sugar and beat until stiff. Beat the yolks until thick and pale yellow; beat in remaining sugar and vanilla extract or framboise. Stir in the melted chocolate and fold in the beaten egg whites. Heavily butter a 10-inch round baking dish or 1½ quart soufflé dish with collar, and sprinkle with about 1 tablespoon sugar, just to coat surface. Spoon in the soufflé mixture. Bake in a preheated 375° oven for 30 to 35 minutes or until set. Meanwhile, purée raspberries in a blender and push through a sieve, discarding seeds. Pour the sauce into a pitcher. Serve soufflé with sauce poured over each serving. Makes 6 servings.

Glorious Strawberry Pie

This is an old-fashioned favorite fruit pie recreated from my Oregon childhood, savoring the wonderful Willamette Valley strawberries.

Butter Tart Shell (see page 222)
5 cups hulled, halved strawberries
⅓ cup boiling water
3 tablespoons honey

*2 tablespoons cornstarch blended
    with 2 tablespoons cold water*
Juice of ½ lemon
*Whipped cream, for garnish,
    optional*

Prepare Butter Tart Shell.

Place berries in a bowl and pour boiling water mixed with 1 tablespoon honey over them. Let stand 1 minute; pour off juices into a small saucepan and add remaining honey, cornstarch mixture, and lemon juice. Bring to a boil and simmer until thickened, stirring constantly. Let cool. Spoon over berries and mix gently. Pile into baked tart shell and cool. Serve cut in wedges and with a dollop of whipped cream, if desired. Makes 6 servings.

Lemon Cheese Tart

Snappy with citrus juice and zest, this French cheese tart is doubly refreshing. Serve it plain or accent it with blueberries, strawberries, or kiwi
fruit arranged on top.

Butter Tart Shell (recipe follows)
1 package (8 ounces) cream cheese
    or 1 cup Yogurt Cheese
    (see page 248)
¾ cup sugar

3 eggs
2 teaspoons grated lemon zest
½ cup lemon juice
Mint sprigs or fruit for topping

Prepare Butter Tart Shell.

Using an electric mixer, beat the cheese until creamy, then beat in the
sugar, eggs, lemon zest, and juice. Pour into baked tart shell and bake in
a preheated 350° oven for 20 minutes or until set. Let cool and chill.
Garnish with mint or fruit. Cut in wedges. Makes 8 servings.

BUTTER TART SHELL:

1 cup flour
8 tablespoons (1 stick) butter
2 tablespoons powdered sugar

With an electric mixer or a food processor fitted with the steel blade, mix
together the flour, butter, and powdered sugar just until particles are
crumbly. Pat into the bottom and up the sides of an 11-inch flan pan with
scalloped sides and removable bottom. Place the tart shell in the freezer
for 10 minutes to firm up. Bake in a 425° oven for 8 to 10 minutes or until
lightly browned.

Banana Sponge Cake Fucilla

Choose overripe bananas to impart a sweet fruity flavor to this ethereal sponge cake. It's a favorite of a wonderful California cook and friend.

7 eggs, separated, and at room
   temperature
1 cup sugar
1 cup mashed ripe bananas

1 cup sifted cake flour
1/8 teaspoon salt
1/2 teaspoon cream of tartar

Beat the egg yolks until they turn lemon colored. Continue beating while adding the sugar a little at a time. Add the mashed bananas and mix well. Sift flour and fold into the egg yolk mixture. Beat the egg whites until frothy. Then add the salt and cream of tartar and continue beating until the whites form stiff, upright peaks. Do not overbeat. Fold the whites into the batter. Turn into an ungreased 10-inch tube pan with removable bottom. Place in a cold oven, turn temperature to 350°, and bake for 50 minutes or until the cake springs back when gently pressed with a finger. Hang upside down in the pan until cold. Remove from pan and serve plain or top it with whipped cream and sliced bananas or berries. Makes 12 servings.

Auntie's Wind Cake

This is a remarkable cake—foolproof and sturdy, yet light. It is superb plain or topped with sliced peaches or nectarines and ice cream.

5 eggs, separated
¾ cup cool water
1½ cups sugar
2 cups cake flour

1 teaspoon vanilla extract
⅛ teaspoon salt
⅛ teaspoon cream of tartar

Beat the egg yolks until light; add water and beat 5 minutes. Add the sugar gradually, beating well. Fold in the flour and vanilla extract. Beat the egg whites until foamy; add salt and cream of tartar and beat until stiff but not dry. Fold egg whites into yolk mixture. Turn into an ungreased 10-inch tube pan. Bake in a preheated 300° oven for 1 hour or until a toothpick inserted comes out clean. Turn upside down to cool. When cold, remove the cake from the pan. Makes 12 servings.

Feathery Chocolate Almond Cake

This light and airy ground nut cake is excellent plain or top it with strawberries, raspberries, sliced peaches or nectarines, and ice cream or frozen yogurt.

1½ cups almonds, filberts, pecans,
    or walnuts
4 ounces semisweet chocolate
5 eggs, separated
⅛ teaspoon salt

⅛ teaspoon cream of tartar
1 cup brown sugar, firmly packed
1 teaspoon vanilla extract
2 teaspoons freshly grated orange
    zest

In a food processor or blender, process the nuts until finely ground and place them in a bowl. Process chocolate until grated; add to the nuts.

In a large bowl, beat the egg whites until foamy, add salt and cream of tartar, and beat until soft peaks form. Beat in 2 tablespoons of the sugar. In another bowl, beat the egg yolks until thick and lemon colored and beat in remaining sugar and vanilla extract. Mix together the nuts, chocolate, and orange zest and fold half of the mixture into the egg yolks. Fold in one-third of the egg whites. Then fold in the remaining nut mixture and lastly fold in remaining egg whites.

Turn batter into an ungreased 9-inch springform pan. Bake in a preheated 350° oven for 30 minutes or until set. Let cool on a rack. Remove pan sides and cut in wedges. Makes 10 to 12 servings.

Chocolate Fantasy Roll

This heavenly chocolate log is surprisingly fast to make. Dust it with powdered sugar or swirl on a glaze to resemble bark.

3 tablespoons unsweetened
   European-style cocoa
1 cup unsifted powdered sugar
1 tablespoon all-purpose flour
⅛ teaspoon salt
5 eggs, separated
⅛ teaspoon cream of tartar

1 teaspoon vanilla extract
Powdered sugar
1 cup heavy cream
2 tablespoons Amaretto, white
   crème de menthe, or Cointreau
Chocolate Glaze (recipe follows,
   optional)

Grease a 10 by 15-inch baking pan, line it with parchment or waxed paper, and butter the paper.

Sift together the cocoa, ¾ cup of the powdered sugar, the flour, and the salt. Beat the egg whites until foamy, add cream of tartar, and beat until soft peaks form. Then beat in the remaining ¼ cup powdered sugar. Set aside.

Beat the egg yolks until thick and lemon colored, add the vanilla extract, and mix in the dry ingredients. Then gently fold in the egg white meringue. Spread the batter evenly in the prepared pan and bake in a preheated 400° oven for 10 minutes, or until the top springs back when touched lightly. Immediately turn out on a towel dusted with powdered sugar and peel off the waxed paper. Roll up and let cool.

Whip cream until stiff and flavor with 1 tablespoon powdered sugar and, if desired, the liqueur. Unroll cake, spread cream filling over it, and roll up again. Chill. If desired spread with Chocolate Glaze. Cut on the diagonal. Makes 6 to 8 servings.

CHOCOLATE GLAZE:

2 ounces semisweet chocolate
1½ tablespoons butter

¼ cup light cream
⅓ cup powdered sugar

In a small saucepan, melt the chocolate with the butter. Add the cream and stir until the mixture is well blended. Remove from heat and beat in the powdered sugar. Let cool until slightly thickened, then spread on top to resemble "bark."

Chocolate Angel Cake

This cocoa-flavored angel cake is a pleasant composite of lightness and richness. Dress it up with a topping of berries and frozen yogurt or ice milk.

1⅔ cups egg whites
    (approximately 14)
1½ teaspoons cream of tartar
½ teaspoon salt
4 teaspoons water

2 cups sugar
1½ teaspoons vanilla extract
1 cup all-purpose flour
6 tablespoons unsweetened pow-
    dered European-style cocoa

Beat the egg whites until frothy and beat in cream of tartar, salt, and water. Beat until soft peaks form and beat in 1¼ cups of the sugar and the vanilla extract. Stir together the flour, remaining ¾ cup sugar, and the cocoa; add to whites and fold in. Turn into an ungreased 10-inch tube pan. Bake in a preheated 400° oven for 10 minutes; reduce heat to 375° and bake 30 minutes longer or until a toothpick inserted comes out clean. Let cool upside down. To serve, remove from pan and slice in wedges. Makes about 14 servings.

Chocolate Almond Torte

A delicious flavor overshadows the homey appearance of this flourless chocolate cake.

6 ounces semisweet chocolate
2 tablespoons double strength
  coffee
5 eggs, separated
Dash cream of tartar

Dash salt
½ cup sugar
¼ cup fine, soft bread crumbs
1 cup ground toasted almonds
½ teaspoon vanilla extract

Melt the chocolate with the coffee in top of double boiler, stirring to blend. Let cool.

Beat egg whites until foamy, add cream of tartar and salt, and beat until soft peaks form. Gradually beat in ¼ cup of the sugar. Beat egg yolks and the remaining ¼ cup sugar until thick and lemon colored. Stir in bread crumbs, almonds, and vanilla extract. Gently stir in chocolate. Fold egg whites into the yolk mixture.

Line a 10-inch springform pan with parchment and pour in the batter, smoothing top evenly. Bake in a preheated 350° oven for 25 to 30 minutes or until just barely done. Let cool on a rack and then remove pan sides. Dust top with powdered sugar shaken through a strainer. Makes 8 to 10 servings.

Orange Pecan Cake

This light, spongy nut cake is excellent served in the old-fashioned way with whipped cream and raspberries, strawberries, or sliced peaches or nectarines. Almonds may also be used instead of the pecans.

5 eggs, separated
2 egg whites
⅛ teaspoon salt
⅛ teaspoon cream of tartar
1 cup granulated sugar

3 tablespoons Amaretto, Frangelico, or orange-flavored liqueur
2 tablespoons grated orange zest
1 cup plus 2 tablespoons flour
¾ cup finely ground pecans or almonds

Place the 7 egg whites in a mixing bowl and beat until foamy. Add salt and cream of tartar and beat until soft peaks form. Gradually add ½ cup of the sugar and continue beating until the whites are stiff but moist. In a separate bowl, beat egg yolks until well blended. Slowly add the remaining sugar and continue beating until the mixture is a very pale yellow. Stir in the liqueur and orange zest. Sift on one-third of the flour and sprinkle on one-third of the ground nuts. Gently fold into the yolk mixture until almost blended. Fold in remaining flour and nuts, half at a time.

Pour into an ungreased 10-inch springform pan with removable bottom. Bake in a preheated 350° oven for 30 to 40 minutes or until a toothpick inserted comes out clean. Remove from oven and invert to cool. When cool, remove pan sides. Slice and serve plain or with whipped cream and fruit, if desired. Makes about 10 servings.

White Chocolate and Pistachio Chipperoos

White chocolate chips and pistachios are an excellent flavor duo in these wholesome cookies. Other nuts may also be used.

8 tablespoons (1 stick) margarine
    or butter
½ cup granulated sugar
¼ cup brown sugar, packed
½ teaspoon vanilla extract
1 egg
1 cup stone-ground flour (see note)

¾ cup oatmeal
½ teaspoon baking soda
¼ teaspoon salt
6 ounces white chocolate chips
½ cup shelled pistachios or
    coarsely chopped almonds,
    walnuts, or pecans

In a bowl, cream together the margarine and sugars until light. Mix in the vanilla extract and egg. Stir together the flour, oatmeal, baking soda, and salt and mix into the creamed mixture until blended. Add chocolate and nuts, mixing well. Drop by teaspoonfuls onto a greased baking sheet. Bake in a preheated 350° oven for 8 to 10 minutes or until golden brown. Makes about 2½ dozen.

Note: If desired use ⅓ cup whole wheat flour and ⅔ cup unbleached flour instead of the 1 cup stone-ground flour.

Triple Ginger Almond Dollars

Three styles of ginger bring an alluring spiciness to these crispy molasses cookies.

10⅔ tablespoons (1 stick plus 2⅔ tablespoons) unsalted butter

1 cup dark brown sugar, firmly packed

¼ cup molasses

1 egg

2¼ cups all-purpose flour

2 teaspoons ground ginger

1 teaspoon baking soda

½ teaspoon salt

2 tablespoons chopped fresh ginger root

⅔ cup finely chopped crystallized ginger

½ cup chopped blanched almonds

In a mixing bowl, cream the butter and sugar until light. Add the molasses and egg and mix until blended. Stir together the flour, ground ginger, baking soda, and salt and add, mixing until blended. Stir in fresh and crystallized ginger and nuts. Cover and chill 1 hour to firm up. Pinch off small pieces of dough and roll into 1-inch balls. Place on a greased baking sheet. Bake in a preheated 350° oven for 10 minutes or until golden brown and set. Remove the cookies to racks to cool. Store in a tightly closed tin. Makes about 4 dozen cookies.

Oatmeal Raisin Crisps

These healthy oatmeal crisps are ideal for a snack at most any time of day.

2 eggs
⅓ cup honey
⅓ cup light brown sugar, firmly
   packed
¼ cup olive oil or canola oil
1 teaspoon vanilla extract
3 tablespoons wheat germ

Zest of 1 orange, julienned
3 cups steel-cut rolled oats
½ cup Muscat raisins or golden
   raisins
¼ cup snipped dried apricots
¼ cup sliced almonds

In a mixing bowl, combine the eggs, honey, brown sugar, olive oil, and vanilla extract. Beat until light and fluffy. Add wheat germ, orange zest, oats, raisins, apricots, and almonds. Let stand 2 hours. Drop from a teaspoon onto greased baking sheets. Using plastic wrap to keep from sticking to the dough, press down each mound of dough making a flat disk. Bake in a preheated 350° oven for 8 minutes or until golden brown. Remove cookies to a rack and let cool. Store in a tightly closed tin. Makes about 32 cookies.

Note: For a sweeter cookie, increase honey and brown sugar to ½ cup each.

Biscotti

This Italian cookie is a perfect keeper; when tightly sealed in a tin it lasts several weeks. A chocolate version is a fancier variation.

3 eggs	*⅞ cup sugar*
1 teaspoon vanilla extract	*1 teaspoon baking soda*
¼ teaspoon almond extract	*Dash salt*
2 cups unbleached flour	*¾ cup toasted whole almonds*

In a small bowl, beat the eggs, vanilla extract, and almond extract with a wire whisk. In a mixing bowl, place flour, sugar, baking soda, and salt. Mix to blend. Add egg mixture and mix until blended, about 1 minute. Mix in nuts.

On a baking sheet lined with aluminum foil, shiny side up, or parchment paper, pat out dough into two logs about 12 inches long, ½ inch high, and 2½ inches wide. Bake in a preheated 300° oven for 50 minutes. Remove from oven and let cool 5 minutes. Slice about ⅜ inch thick, cutting diagonally. Lay cut side down and return to a 275° oven for 30 minutes or until toasted. Store in a tightly closed tin. Makes about 3½ dozen.

VARIATIONS:

Chocolate Glaze. Melt 3 ounces semisweet chocolate and spread over tops of cookies.

Chocolate Biscotti. Reduce flour to 1¾ cups and add ⅓ cup cocoa and 1 tablespoon instant coffee powder to dry mix. Stir to blend. If desired, use toasted diced almonds instead of whole almonds.

Chocolate Almond Wafers

Chocolate speckles this crispy butter wafer for a delightful accompaniment to fruit or ice cream.

1 cup whole almonds
3 ounces semisweet chocolate
8 tablespoons (1 stick) butter, at
  room temperature
⅓ cup brown sugar, firmly packed

1 teaspoon vanilla extract
1 egg
1 cup unbleached or whole wheat
  flour

Grind the almonds in a blender or food processor until they are the consistency of cornmeal and put them into a mixing bowl. Place the chocolate in a blender or food processor and process until grated. Add chocolate to the almonds.

In a mixing bowl, combine the butter and sugar until creamy and beat in vanilla extract and egg. Add the flour, nuts, and chocolate and mix just until dough is blended. Turn out on waxed paper or plastic wrap and shape into a cylinder about 2¼ inches in diameter. Wrap securely and chill until firm, 2 to 3 hours. Slice as thinly as possible, about ⅛ inch thick, and place on a baking sheet. Bake in a preheated 350° oven for 8 minutes or until lightly browned. Makes about 3 dozen.

Toasted Almond Macaroons

These chewy Italian cookies are a wonderful partner to a fresh fruit bowl.

1 can (8 ounces) almond paste   *2 egg whites*
⅞ cup sugar   *½ cup toasted slivered almonds*

In a food processor fitted with the steel blade, place the almond paste, sugar, and egg whites and process until blended. Add almonds and process just to distribute them. Cover baking sheets with parchment or brown paper. Drop rounded teaspoons of batter onto baking sheet, spacing them a few inches apart. Bake in a preheated 325° oven for about 25 minutes or until lightly browned and cooked through. Let cool and remove from paper. If the macaroons stick, moisten the back of the paper to release them. Makes about 3 dozen cookies.

Danish Marzipan Wafers

These crispy almond wafers are a perfect sweet with fruit, ice cream, or frozen yogurt.

5⅓ tablespoons butter
¼ cup almond paste
⅓ cup sugar
1 egg yolk

1 cup all-purpose flour
1 egg, lightly beaten
Granulated sugar, for topping
Sliced almonds

Beat the butter and almond paste until creamy, then beat in the ⅓ cup sugar and egg yolk. Mix in flour to make a smooth dough. On a lightly floured board, roll the dough out about ¼ inch thick. Cut out with a 1½-inch round scalloped cutter. Place rounds on a buttered baking sheet and brush with lightly beaten egg white. Sprinkle with sugar and almonds. Bake in a preheated 350° oven for 10 minutes or until lightly browned. Let cool and store in a covered container. Makes about 2 dozen wafers.

Lemon Tile Cookies

Tile-shaped lemon cookies are a wonderful crispy accompaniment to fruit, custards, ice cream, or frozen yogurt.

3½ tablespoons soft butter
½ cup sugar
2 egg whites
5 tablespoons cake flour
⅓ cup blanched almonds, finely
  ground

¼ teaspoon lemon extract
1 teaspoon freshly ground lemon
  zest
3 tablespoons slivered almonds

Beat together the butter and sugar until light and fluffy. Add the egg whites and beat a few seconds more. Sift the flour, measure again, and stir it into the batter all at once. Fold in the ground almonds, lemon extract, and lemon zest. Butter a baking sheet. Drop batter by half-teaspoonfuls at least 4 inches apart. Spread into 3-inch circles. (Batter will be thin and open in spots.) Sprinkle with a few slivered almonds. Bake in a preheated 425° oven for 4 minutes or until golden brown. Remove from baking sheets immediately and drape over a slender rolling pin, forming a "tile" shape. Repeat with remaining batter. Makes 2 dozen cookies.

Hint: Cookies may be made several days in advance and stored in an airtight container.

Golden Raisin Rum Brownies

Plumped raisins lend a fruity sweetness to these moist brownies.

½ cup golden raisins
¼ cup dark rum
8 tablespoons (1 stick) butter
4 ounces unsweetened chocolate
1 ounce semisweet chocolate
3 eggs

1¼ cups sugar
1 teaspoon vanilla extract
1 cup all-purpose flour
Dash salt
½ cup pistachios or chopped
    pecans

Soak the raisins in rum for 20 minutes. Place the butter and chocolates in the top part of a double boiler and melt over hot water; stir to blend, then cool slightly. Beat the eggs until thick and lemon-colored and gradually beat in the sugar. Stir in chocolate-butter mixture, vanilla, flour, and salt, mixing just until blended. Mix in nuts, raisins, and rum. Pour into a buttered and floured 9-inch square pan. Bake in a preheated 350° oven for 25 minutes, or until set but still moist. Let cool, then cut into squares. Makes about 24.

Double Fudge Brownies

Chocolate bits dot these melt-in-your-mouth brownies that are elegant served slightly warm.

2 ounces unsweetened chocolate
8 tablespoons (1 stick) butter
2 eggs
1 cup sugar
½ teaspoon vanilla extract
½ cup all-purpose flour

Dash salt
½ teaspoon baking powder
½ cup chopped pecans or walnuts
½ cup semisweet chocolate bits
Powdered sugar

Melt the chocolate and butter in the top of a double boiler; stir to blend, then cool. Beat eggs until thick and lemon colored and beat in sugar and vanilla extract. Mix in cooled chocolate and butter. Stir together the flour, salt, and baking powder; add to chocolate mixture and blend well. Stir in nuts and chocolate bits. Turn into a buttered and floured 9-inch square baking pan. Bake in a preheated 350° oven for 20 to 25 minutes or until barely set. Dust with powdered sugar. Let cool, then cut into squares. Makes about 1½ dozen.

House Staples

Certain house favorites are smart to keep on hand, in quantity. A Fruit and Nut Granola is a welcome cereal mix on yogurt at breakfast or as an appealing snack. Yogurt Cheese is a healthful adjunct to the diet, as it enhances whole-grain breakfast toast spread with preserves or marmalade or goes into various dips and spreads.

In season, Oven Dried Tomatoes are easy to prepare and make a welcome condiment for an appetizer, pizza, or pasta. For a homey touch, try Strawberry Preserves and Orange Marmalade. Make them with ease on a weekend, then store in the freezer for use year-round.

Blue Cheese Spread

A zippy blue cheese spread makes a suave sauce to melt into baked potatoes or barbecued steak, hamburgers, or ground turkey burgers.

2 ounces blue or Roquefort cheese
½ cup Yogurt Cheese
   (see page 248)
2 shallots, minced

1 clove garlic, minced
1 teaspoon fresh tarragon, chopped
   or ¼ teaspoon dried tarragon
2 tablespoons dry vermouth

Beat together until creamy the cheese, Yogurt Cheese, shallots, garlic, tarragon, and vermouth. Spoon into a bowl, cover, and chill until serving time. Makes enough for 3 to 4 servings.

Pesto Sauce

This robust Italian herb sauce is excellent for pasta, soups, vegetables, and topping crusty toast or pizza. Prepare in quantity and freeze.

2 cups packed basil leaves
3 cloves garlic, minced
3 tablespoons olive oil
¼ cup dry Monterey Jack or
  Parmesan cheese

¼ teaspoon freshly ground pepper
¼ cup pine nuts, walnuts, or
  pistachios

Place the basil, garlic, olive oil, cheese, pepper, and nuts in a food processor fitted with the steel blade. Process until finely blended. Turn into a container, cover, and chill or freeze. Makes about 1½ cups.

Swiss Buttered Herb Sauce

Let this sprightly herb sauce drench baked potatoes, green beans, steak, or grilled salmon.

¼ cup butter
1 anchovy fillet, chopped
1 teaspoon Dijon mustard
1 teaspoon lemon juice
6 tablespoons finely chopped
    Italian parsley

2 shallots, finely chopped
1 clove garlic, minced
1½ teaspoons chopped chives or
    green onion tops

In a small saucepan, heat together the butter, anchovies, mustard, and lemon juice. When melted, remove from heat and stir in parsley, shallots, garlic, and chives. Spoon hot over vegetables or meats. Makes 4 servings.

Salsa

This hot chili salsa makes a vibrant accent on tacos, grilled meats, chicken, and fish. Vary the heat level to suit your taste.

3 firm, ripe tomatoes, peeled, seeded, and chopped
1 small sweet red or white onion, finely chopped
1 small green chili pepper, seeded and chopped or 2 to 3 tablespoons chopped canned green chiles

Salt and pepper, to taste
½ teaspoon sugar
2 tablespoons cilantro, chopped

In a bowl, mix together the tomatoes, onion, chili pepper, salt, pepper, sugar, and cilantro. Cover and chill 1 hour for flavors to blend. Makes about 3 cups.

Versatile Fruit Salsa

This ginger and lime-zested fruit salsa can be made with a variety of fresh fruits.

2 cups diced mango, papaya,
  nectarines, or peaches
½ cup diced red onion
½ cup diced red pepper

¼ cup chopped cilantro
2 tablespoons lime juice
2 teaspoons grated ginger root
Dash chili powder (optional)

Place the mango, red onion, red pepper, cilantro, lime juice, grated ginger root, and chili powder (if desired) in a bowl. Mix lightly. Cover and chill until serving time. Makes about 4 servings.

Lemon Pistachio Sauce

This piquant nut sauce is excellent on a variety of hot or cold cooked vegetables such as Italian green beans, cauliflower, broccoli, fennel, and leeks.

*Zest of ½ lemon, cut in julienne
    pieces*
2 tablespoons pistachios

2 anchovy fillets
1 tablespoon walnut oil
1 teaspoon white wine vinegar

On a board, chop together the lemon zest, nuts, and anchovies until finely minced. Place in a small bowl and stir in the oil and vinegar. Makes about ¼ cup sauce, enough for 4 servings.

Yogurt Cheese

Either homemade yogurt or commercial yogurt prepared without gelatin can be used for this basic, healthy cheese.

1 quart plain low-fat yogurt without gelatin

Use either a colander lined with a double thickness of cheesecloth or a regular cheesemaker strainer. Place the colander or strainer over a deep casserole or bowl and spoon in the yogurt. Cover with plastic wrap and refrigerate about 24 hours or until the cheese is as thick as desired. Scoop the cheese into a container and cover. Discard the liquid that remains. Use the Yogurt Cheese as desired. Keeps refrigerated about 3 to 4 days. Makes about 1¾ cups.

Couscous-Stuffed Grape Leaves

Grape leaves stuffed with herb-scented couscous are fast to assemble.

¾ cup couscous
1 cup boiling water
2 tablespoons lemon juice
2 tablespoons olive oil
2 teaspoons grated lemon zest
2 green onions, chopped
½ teaspoon allspice

¼ teaspoon freshly ground black
  pepper
⅓ cup chopped parsley
3 tablespoons chopped fresh basil
3 to 4 dozen canned grape leaves,
  rinsed
1 pint cherry tomatoes
Lemon wedges

Place couscous in a bowl and pour boiling water over it; let stand until cooled to room temperature. For the dressing, stir together the lemon juice, oil, lemon zest, green onions, allspice, pepper, parsley, and basil. Pour over the couscous and fluff it with a fork. Chill. Arrange grape leaves on a flat surface, shiny side down. Place a tablespoon of couscous at the stem end. Fold like an envelope and roll up. Place on a platter. Garnish with cherry tomatoes and lemon wedges. Makes 3 to 4 dozen.

Fruit and Nut Granola

This toasty granola is very lightly enriched with honey and olive oil, making it a healthy snack.

3 tablespoons honey
2 tablespoons olive oil
¼ cup water
¼ teaspoon almond extract
1 teaspoon vanilla extract
2 cups old-fashioned oats

2 tablespoons wheat germ
2 tablespoons oat bran
¼ cup snipped dried apricots
3 tablespoons light or dark raisins
¼ cup sliced almonds

Place the honey, oil, and water in a saucepan and bring to a boil. Remove from heat and stir in almond and vanilla extracts. Add oats, wheat germ, and bran and stir until coated. Turn into a baking pan. Bake in a 300° oven for 20 minutes, stirring once or twice. Add apricots, raisins, and almonds and continue baking 10 minutes longer, stirring once or twice. Let cool and store in an airtight container. Makes about 2½ cups.

Gingered Cranberry Relish

This fresh tangy fruit relish is superb with barbecued meats and roast turkey or chicken. When cranberries are in season, stash them away in the freezer for handy use later.

2 oranges
2 Granny Smith apples, quartered
   and cored
1 package (12 ounces) whole
   cranberries

1 tablespoon chopped fresh ginger
   root
⅓ cup sugar

With a vegetable peeler, peel zest from the oranges; set aside. Peel off and discard the white pith and cut oranges into sixths. Place half of the oranges, half the orange zest, half the apples, along with all of the cranberries, the ginger root, and the sugar in the food processor fitted with the steel blade. Process until finely chopped. Turn out into a container. Put the remaining ingredients in the food processor and process until finely chopped. Add to the cranberry mixture and mix to combine. Cover and chill 4 hours before serving. Keeps refrigerated 3 or 4 days. Makes about 1½ quarts.

Apricot Chutney

A tangy ginger chutney makes a great accompaniment to grilled food or curries.

8 cups diced, peeled, firm apricots   *2 teaspoons mustard seeds*
1 large onion, chopped   *1½ teaspoons salt*
2 cloves garlic, chopped   *2 sticks cinnamon*
¼ cup chopped fresh ginger root   *1 teaspoon ground cardamom*
¾ cup brown sugar, firmly packed   *1 teaspoon allspice*
1½ cups cider vinegar   *Tiny piece red pepper*

Combine the above ingredients in a large pot and simmer until fruit is translucent and thick, about 30 minutes. Makes about 6 half-pints.

Note: If desired, store in the freezer.

Orange Marmalade

It's well worth the effort to make this tangy marmalade loaded with chewy peel. You must have a scale to weigh the fruit in order to add the proper amount of sugar.

7 large navel oranges   *1 cup lemon juice*
Zest of 7 additional oranges   *Sugar*

Wash and peel the oranges. Place the zest of the 14 oranges in a saucepan, barely cover with water, and simmer 25 minutes, covered. Reserve the cooking water. Using a grapefruit knife, slip off the stringy white part of the orange peel, but do not make the peel too thin. Slice julienne style. Remove strings from oranges and slice fruit thinly. Place in a pan, add zest and the water in which zest was cooked. Add lemon juice and let sit half an hour. Cover and simmer 25 minutes or until mushy. Add an equal weight of the fruit in sugar and stir to combine. When dissolved, bring to a boil and place in two pans, if necessary. Boil while stirring for 8 minutes. If two pots were used, combine marmalade in one large pot and let sit for half a day, stirring occasionally. Ladle into glasses and seal. Makes about 12 half pints.

Strawberry Preserves

Plump strawberries are bound in a runny scarlet jelly for these delicious preserves to top breads and ice cream.

4 cups sugar
⅔ cup water

4 cups strawberries
½ cup lemon juice

Boil sugar and water together a few minutes to make a thick syrup. Wash berries, hull, and toss together lightly with lemon juice but do not crush. Add a few berries at a time to the boiling syrup; keeping syrup boiling all the time. When all berries are added, continue boiling 15 to 20 minutes or until thick. Pour preserves into a shallow pan and let stand 24 hours, shaking pan occasionally. Pour into hot sterilized jars and seal. Makes 4 half-pints.

Oven-Dried Tomatoes

Oven-drying your own tomatoes is so easy and makes a versatile condiment for an appetizer, a pizza or pasta topping, or a garnish for entrées.

4 pounds red plum or Roma tomatoes, washed and stemmed
2 teaspoons salt

Cut tomatoes in half, leaving the two sides attached. Overlap two wire racks on large 10 by 15-inch baking sheets and cover with cheesecloth. Arrange tomatoes, cut side up, on the racks and sprinkle lightly with salt. Place in a preheated 200° oven and let dry until shriveled yet still flexible, about 8 to 14 hours, depending on the size of the tomatoes. Place in a brown paper bag and let stand at room temperature a day for the moisture to equalize. Then package in sealable plastic bags or jars and freeze. Let thaw and store in the refrigerator while using. Makes about 1 pint.

Index